PNЯ253

VOLUME 46   NUMBER 5   MAY – JUNE 2

Editorial

'For now, though, we need to ensure we protect as much of our cultural ecology as we can – and as things stand, every part of it is in peril. While our National Portfolio Organisations may appear to be relatively well-funded, they generally depend on very high levels of earned income, which have disappeared overnight. That, combined with relatively small levels of reserves, has meant that many National Portfolio Organisations have already been placed in real jeopardy by this crisis. Some may not survive. And while individually the failure of these organisations would be painful, collectively their loss would decimate our cultural infrastructure. Together, they employ thousands of people, commission thousands more, and support many small companies through their supply chains.'

Darren Henley, Arts Council England Chief Executive, 31 March 2020

When *PN Review* 252 was mailed out to subscribers a couple of months ago, Covid-19 still seemed some way off. On 11 January China announced the first death in Wuhan. Less than a week later a case was reported in Thailand. On 23 January the WHO said the outbreak did not constitute an international public emergency. Seven days later, global emergency was declared. By 6 February Europe had 30 confirmed cases.

Time seemed to accelerate, and then grind to a halt. A general sense of urgency as we were propelled towards lockdown, and then – lockdown. Now, as I write, in the fourth week of that lockdown, we seem to have stuck fast in a spell. News programmes recite alarming numbers, remind us of our ignorance of the foe that now controls us, and provide a wealth of more or less informed hypotheses and prophecies about what might happen if this, or if that, and when. Much grieving is reported, and much human kindness. Will the UK become the worst-afflicted country in Europe, will the lock-down be extended, or eased, and if so by what means? Other important news has been driven out by rumour and authoritative suppositions. The discourse of current affairs is dangerously poor in significant facts and is largely conducted in what Christine Brooke-Rose explored so tellingly in her novel *Amalgamemnon* (1984): non-realised tenses. Not Wordsworth's promise, 'something evermore about to be', not the huge figures of the Apocalypse itself, but those invisible, minute viruses working their way like ironies through the populations of the world, adjusting consciousness and imagination.

The *PN Review* submissions portal has been exposed to Covid-19. Not a day passes without coronavirus poems filling it up. As one friend wrote, 'Gather ye soapsuds while ye may.' Even analeptically. *The Times* (12 April) quotes University of Glasgow Professor Gerry Carruthers, 'Edwin Morgan would have written a fantastic poem about the coronavirus.' 'Edwin Morgan would have written' – there is Brooke-Rose's non-realised tense at work. Supposition has gathered a kind of spurious authority. *The Times* reflects that Morgan himself, a decade dead, is nonetheless a victim of the pandemic: celebrations of his centenary have been entirely disrupted.

Poetry magazines, so long as their printers stay in business and the post office keeps delivering, are so far the least Covid-19-vulnerable operations in the poetry world. Their lives change because editorial and design staff work remotely, and because the lockdown gives poets a tremendous opportunity to send work, and more and more work. What was an imposing backlog of submissions begins to loom in a more sinister way.

But the rest of the poetry world's ecology is entirely changed.

Soon after lockdown was declared, a number of commercial and specialist publishers altered their forward schedules, some cancelling their spring and summer lists, some delaying lead titles. Without bookshops, the decision was logical. A number of employees were furloughed. The longer-term consequences on those companies' schedules, cash-flow and reach will require imaginative handling. The calendar remains unhelpfully inelastic.

Certainly the wholesale cancellation of literary festivals and events has driven a coach and horses through publishers' promotional programmes. Poetry launches and events, if they are to continue, must find new means. Publishers must invent ways of selling books in quantity in the absence of bookshops. Social media, long crucial in informing and promoting books, have rapidly to adapt and become primary sales media as well, complicating their friendly informality. The on-line launch event is one of a number of evolving tools which stand in for the physical poet, the physical audience and the physical bookseller. If poetry audiences prove (temporarily) content with on-line presentations, will readership find its way to these events? Will people buy books on line? If so, the damage to the business of contemporary poetry may be contained. It seems likely that techniques developed in this period will remain in place after restrictions are lifted. By their means we will have reached readers and writers who before we may have missed, including the disabled and deaf, and a wide international constituency. But here we too risk the use of non-realised tenses.

One *fact* is unarguable. As soon as the implications of the pandemic were clear, Arts Council England took immediate steps to reassure and support its always vulnerable sector. They contacted clients – individuals and organisations – offering a well-thought-out series of initiatives ('our Covid-19 Emergency Response Package') to support clients' staff and work. As a consequence, there was immediately, within the Arts sector, a sense of common cause. Having rallied us in this way, the Arts Council has continued to encourage and advise. Despite the crisis, it is possible to feel optimistic about outcomes. Guidance, blogs by members of the 'leadership team', suggestions of help available from local and national government, and initiatives with the BBC and others, are fully detailed. Some of clients' reporting requirements were relaxed. It felt – it feels – as though we are collaborating, however different our enterprises, in a joined-up campaign. It includes National Portfolio Organisations and new initiatives.

At a time when theatres, concert halls, galleries, bookshops and venues are closed, this support will help the arts sector back to viability when restrictions are lifted and we move forward into the new normal, whatever it may be.

News & Notes

Script of Storms · *Marius Kociejowski reports:* On 14 February 2020 Michael Hersch (*PNR*'s composer in residence) had his premiere of *The Script of Storms*, his setting for orchestra and soprano of poems by the late Fawzi Karim whose two collections *Plague Lands and other poems* (2011) and *Incomprehensible Lesson* (2019) are published by Carcanet. Tito Muñoz conducted the BBC Symphony Orchestra at Maida Vale Studios with soprano Ah Young Hong taking on the extreme challenges of a work that was not exactly Valentine's Day fare. Hersch, the most poetry-driven of composers, set some of the darkest passages in Karim's work including an instance of *sahel*, 'The Iraqi Revolution's guillotine' – a scene the poet witnessed as a child in Baghdad – which comprises dragging a mutilated corpse through the streets. Almost dead centre in the 20-minute work are two short lines where both poet and composer simultaneously fix their respective positions: 'Me this, isolate sculpture. I'm cold. / My plinth is the void.' Attending the concert was English composer David Hackbridge Johnson who in *PNR* 250 wrote an appreciation of Hersch's *Zwischen Leben und Tod*. Johnson, although he comes from a wholly different sonic world, spoke deeply of *The Script of Storms* in a series of visual images – the gift seems his alone – in which he notes 'a landscape that appears still and blanched. And then flocks of birds rise up in a paroxysm of cries and frantic wings... The way the double basses suddenly have a two-note tune that aches gutturally as if straining from a swamp; its neck taut with the effort of utterance. Those twisted fanfares in the brass as if an entire regimental band is being crushed in a fist. And the voice, like a mother at the foot of a bloodstained wall.' Prior to the performance, Hersch spoke movingly of his friendship with the poet and how, upon hearing Ah Young Hong for the first time, Karim, perhaps the only Arab to have written extensively on western classical music, became obsessed with the progress of a composition that would serve as a vehicle for her remarkable voice. It was striking to observe how the most painful moments in his poems were delivered in high, piercing notes that seemed to obliterate the words themselves as if their fullest expression were not allowable. Sadly, Fawzi Karim did not live to hear the work, but his family was in attendance.

A National Poetry Centre · On 27 February the Poet Laureate, Simon Armitage, announced ambitious plans for a National Poetry Centre in Leeds. Andrew Motion's legacy was the wonderful Poetry Archive. This will be Armitage's legacy, to his native Yorkshire and to the nation. He intends that poetry should be recognised in line with other national art forms that have physical headquarters and venues, for example the National Theatre and the National Gallery. The National Poetry Centre will be a collaboration led by Leeds City Council, Leeds 2023, the University of Leeds and other partners. It will provide a public space that includes an extensive poetry collection with research facilities, rehearsal and performance spaces, a café, and gatherings and events. One hopes it may also accommodate a dedicated Poetry Bookshop stocking books, journals and other poetry publications.

'In my view,' the Laureate declared, 'the centre needs to be outside London and Leeds is an ideal location: accessible, central, dynamic, contemporary, future-minded, people-oriented, community-aware, committed to cultural regeneration, and building momentum towards 2023. [...] Poetry is one of our most ancient and proudest artistic endeavours, steeped in tradition, history and ritual; it's also undergoing,' he declares, 'an incredible renaissance at present, particularly in relation to new generations of writers and performers across diverse backgrounds who have found in poetry a way of articulating their concerns and expressing their feelings.' Leeds 2023 creative director Kully Thiarai set a target: 'We intend that the new centre will be open in time for our spectacular year of culture in 2023.'

Further news on the Laureate · He began (on 11 March) presenting a series of Radio 4 podcasts on BBC Sounds entitled 'The Poet Laureate has Gone to his Shed', taking with him a range of artists (one hopes the shed is sufficiently large to allow for social distancing). We are enjoined to, 'Listen in on BBC Sounds as some of the best creative talents share their writing secrets and life lessons with Simon, nestled at the bottom of his garden. [...] Over 12 episodes guests include acclaimed spoken word performer Kate Tempest, Turner Prize recipient Antony Gormley, model and actress Lily Cole, DJ and Elbow frontman Guy Garvey, actress Maxine Peake, poet Jackie Kay, and world-record beat-boxing champion Testament. Sam Lee – Mercury Prize short listed folk singer – tries to get Armitage out of the shed to join one of his trips in the woods to sing with Nightingales, and Trinidadian judge Melanie Plimmer casts a judicious eye over the arguments of the two poetic birds.'

Struck by history · The Pulitzer Prize-winning poet Lisel Mueller (born Elisabeth Neumann) died in Chicago in February at the age of ninety-six. One of her themes was her flight from Nazi Germany with her family when she was fifteen. She was awarded the Pulitzer in 1997 for *Alive Together: New and Selected Poems*. By then she was thirty-two years into her career as a university teacher and published poet, writing in what was, after all, a second language which she mastered with a kind of deliberate precision that makes the writing unusually defined. In one of her best-loved poems, 'Bach Transcribing Vivaldi', she writes:

> One asked the road to the land of the golden lion
> whose eyes never weep, whose lifted hand scepters
> the seasons of stars and the grafting of generations;
> the other searched from the kingdom of the lamb
> with the trembling fleece, whose live unreasoning heart
> consumes the mortal treasures of his loves.

Late in 2019 she was awarded the *Bundesverdienstkreuz* – the Order of Merit of the Federal Republic of Germany. In her powerful prose poem, in numbered paragraphs, 'Curriculum Vitae', she remembers how, 'My country was struck by history more deadly than earthquakes or hurricanes.' Later, arriving in the new country, 'In the new language everyone spoke too fast. Eventually I caught up with them.' Later still, 'One day, on a crowded elevator, everyone's face was younger than mine.'

Sometimes Gladness · John Kinsella wrote in the *Guardian* of Australian poet Bruce Dawe, who died in April at the age of 90. Les Murray had dubbed him 'our great master of applied poetry', and he was regarded by some as the most influential poet Australia had produced, partly because of his place in the curriculum, so that few Australians remain innocent of him. Kinsella stressed the diversity of Dawe's readership. 'This diversity would have mattered to him. His work was widely honoured in his lifetime, including with the Patrick White award and a Christopher Brennan award for lifetime achievement in poetry. From a working-class background with broken schooling in Melbourne, then later ongoing commitment to part-time education, through to receiving a PhD, he eventually became a teacher and academic in Queensland. Dawe's earlier work experience (his many jobs included being a postman, working in a battery factory and serving for a long period with the RAAF) provided the "lived life" feel of social familiarity in his poems.' And Kinsella remembered how, 'For decades, when you went into a second-hand bookshop in Australia, even if there was no poetry section, you'd find at least one book of poetry, and that book would be Bruce Dawe's *Sometimes Gladness*. It wasn't simply about a discarded book looking for a new owner, but the inevitable circulation of a school standard across the country. Innumerable copies of the many (updated) editions of this timeless classic were in high-school kids' bags, lockers, bookcases, desks and maybe scattered on their floors after a heavy study session.'

The Brazen Plagiarist · *Evan Jones writes:* The poet Kiki Dimoula has died. Born in Athens in 1931, she met the poet Athos Dimoulas (1921–85) while in high-school and they had two children together. She worked for many years at the Bank of Athens before quitting in 1974. Her books began appearing in the 1950s and she became that rare thing: a popular, well-read poet. Her individual poetry collections sold regularly in the area of ten thousand copies, and in 2002, she became the first woman elected to the Chair in Poetry at the Academy of Athens (only a handful of women have been elected to the Academy since its founding in 1926 – Dimoula was the third). Her discreet, metaphysical poems, full of sharp syntactical switches and energy, focus on the quotidian – very different from the mythopoetic world that readers associate with the major Modernist Modern Greek poets – even as they engage deeply with the history of the Greek language. Yale University Press published a dual-language selection of her poems, *The Brazen Plagiarist,* in 2012, translated by Cecile Inglessis Margellos and Rika Lesser. And Gallimard published a French translation by Michel Volkovitch in 2010, making Dimoula the first female poet ever to be included in their poetry series. She died aged eighty-nine in hospital, Saturday 22 February 2020, after a long illness.

Marks of Desire, Not of Doubt: Desdemona In Action

VAHNI CAPILDEO

Writing from Milan in 1880, Boito, Verdi's librettist for *Otello*, compares the atmosphere of Shakespeare's tragedy to a 'room where two people are about to die of asphyxiation'. Anxious to steer Verdi away from conventional theatricality, Boito overemphasizes his desire to 'seal' Desdemona and Othello in this 'lethal chamber'. William Weaver's translation of the correspondence is uncomfortable to read during the days of lockdown in which this piece is written. The government of Trinidad and Tobago (where I happen to be), led by a Prime Minister who is qualified volcanologist with training in disaster preparedness, has taken a strong, clear, firm stance on quarantine to flatten the curve of the spread of the coronavirus. Only essential travel is permitted. Food retailers and delivery services have been closed, putting the itinerant poor, and the medically housebound, at a disadvantage. Post is being sorted and held, not distributed, except for welfare cheques. The geckos chirrup ever more loudly from their concealed runs between the ceiling and the roof. The invisible neighbour is known to be contributing to the sewing of a thousand home-made protective masks, for charity. It is illegal to walk unmasked, which probably contradicts the old colonial law, still on the books, which makes it illegal to walk masked. Is it a type of escape, then, at the end of this paragraph, to ascend what Verdi himself called the 'rickety scale' of his Desdemona's 'Ave Maria', and contemplate sopranos singing about heaven?

It is no kind of escape to consider the meaning of consent, and enthusiastic and active consent is what the 'Ave Maria' celebrates. Shakespeare's Desdemona sings no such song. His heroine is both imprisoned in Marian imagery, and damned as a whore. Michael Cassio, the Florentine wrongly suspected of being her adulterous lover, makes these comparisons with irritating intensity. In Act II, scene i, as storms of weather and storms of war accompany Desdemona to Cyprus, Cassio, describing Desdemona as a 'maid' excelling all possible praise, who 'in th'essential vesture of creation / Does tire the [ingener]', echoes the angel's salutation to Mary in the Gospel of St Luke. Shakespeare makes sure nobody misses the allusion. He makes Cassio greet his general's wife: 'Hail to thee, lady! And the grace of heaven / Before, behind thee, and on every hand, / Enwheel thee round!' Cassio joins the extensive company of people in the play who reject plain speech, preferring to exalt, overblow, overspecify, whinge, curse, degrade or lie. This widespread refusal of everyday language is the context for the impossibility of conducting an everyday marriage. The rhetoricalization of her identity seems to trap Desdemona. If she is not enskied, she must be fallen.

Verdi's genius, in composing an 'Ave Maria' for the soprano who plays Desdemona, is that the character is not thereby further divinized. She becomes, if anything, a more turbulent vector of the play's tensions. Moreover, she wins the stage, doing what none of the men can. In Verdi's setting, the singer shines by showing off physical resilience and athletic lung power. First murmuring or muttering her devotions on one note in a display of technical control as she finishes the first half of the text, she proceeds to ascend vocal heights. The sound is ethereal; its muscular production is not – and the shape of the aria suggests that Desdemona is determined to go where she is going. Verdi and Boito strengthen the sense that Desdemona is an original: they then disrupt the expected wording of the 'Ave Maria', interpolating Desdemona's personal prayers. Like Dan Burley's twentieth-century American playlet, where a Harlem jive Desdemona spiels all kinds of ungovernable, vivid things, the nineteenth-century opera demonstrates how very much alive, and not pallid, this Venetian girl can be. She elaborates the normal plea for us sinners into a reflection on complicity in violence, and the need for compassion for weak and strong alike. What she notices, and the notes she sings, are busy with real-world detail, not wafting off on a cloud of calm. In effect, she has withheld her consent from being the queenly figure that courtiers would praise, or a frail foreign wife in a hot, dangerous little island. Even meditating, she remains a soldier's companion and match.

That agency and consent are matters of cultural understanding and access, and embodied being, becomes evident in the way verbal communication is patterned, tattered, and tormented by its insufficiency, in Shakespeare's words no less than in Verdi and Boito's words and music. In Shakespeare's Act IV Scene i, Othello's assimilated alien status in Venetian society is exploited by Iago, who teaches him false versions of body language. Othello is fooled by Iago in the way only a sensitive stranger could be fooled: by misinformation about customs and decorum. When Iago hints that Desdemona may indulge quite normally in unauthorized kissing, lying naked in bed with a male friend, and borrowing handkerchiefs, what is perhaps most bewildering is that Iago juggles the descriptions about, as if these activities could be placed on the same plane. I have learnt too well,

from my own experience of emigration and travel, that where everyday behaviour needs to be studied and decoded, it is hard to see *how* to understand, let alone what is happening. Othello is not necessarily credulous. He may simply have taken one of the risks outsiders have to take in order to participate in 'normality', and trusted that Iago, who had proved solid in military engagements, would also be supportive in social environments.

Othello consents to be guided by Iago, who promptly encourages him to snoop on a conversation in which Cassio will reveal his adultery with Desdemona. Iago prepares Othello for snooping by offering a false crib-sheet of body language. In Shakespeare's script, Iago invites Othello to 'mark the fleers, the gibes, and notable scorns, / That dwell in every region of his [Cassio's] face'. He makes the physicality of Othello's officer uncomradely, riddling, no longer something the men (who must have trained together) can in any way share. Like is re-presented as unlike. When Verdi and Boito set this scene, their Iago and Cassio laugh together lightly in a major key duet, reinforcing an illusory likeness between them, and Otello's new and painful sense of difference. The rapid exchanges of their superficial music stand in for a fluent sociality. Otello's exclusion is made evident in the lurching phrases he exclaims to himself. Their kind of banter is not in his repertoire. He cannot join in, and his phrases are unanswerable. Sickening swoops of voice indicate a gradual loss of self-control. His music conveys his diminished ability to exercise reasonable agency.

Returning to Shakespeare's play, the following scene (IV. ii.) sees Othello scrutinizing Desdemona: 'Let me see your eyes; / Look in my face.' For him, at this point, no kind of ocular proof is a true reading. Her body language will be refracted through the devil's dictionary Iago taught him to apply to Cassio's features. Desdemona does not consent to being interpreted. Asking 'What horrible fancy's this?', she relegates Othello's examination to a type of brain-sickness. She exercises her agency against what is by now a huge build-up of symbolic pressure, enacting the free yet devoted wife she signed up to be.

Desdemona's agency tends to be under-read, when her physicality is misread according to later, secular canons of femininity and oppression. Whenever she kneels, it is not merely as a suppliant subject. Her choice to invoke the body language of theologically conceived obedience is a choice which indicates her status as a rational creature, aligned with divine power. When she says, 'I understand a fury in your words. / But not the words' (and the 'fury' should be taken seriously, as a displacement of Othello's better self), this is her diagnosis of his condition; it is not her confession of a lapse in her understanding. To point out the split in expression which lets mood annihilate meaning is to re-implicate the potential for integrity. Like the successful interracial, intercultural lovers in Vidyan Ravintharan's *The Million-petalled Flower of Being Here* (Bloodaxe, 2019), Desdemona is a believer in the imagination. Isolated on an island, in a drama of claustrophobia, she is the spirit of a more than passive resistance. She guards the possibility of a healed and salvific lexicon: the speech that was hers and Othello's at first, in Shakespeare, but which Boito omits and Verdi compensates for – loving and mutual, enthusiastic and active, consenting to be shareable, and shared.

Ernesto Cardenal, 1905–2020

GREVEL LINDOP

The little man with the receding chin, stubbly white beard and dark blue beret didn't make an impressive figure. Until he climbed to the podium and blinked around, settling first his glasses and then his papers, I didn't realise that this was Ernesto Cardenal. When he began to read, in a grainy but musical voice – there was a slight mumble in the enunciation – the effect rapidly became hypnotic. There was a rhythm, a musical pitch, and a sincerity that explained why the Granada International Poetry Festival of that year (it was 2013) was being held in his honour.

Cardenal, who died at the age of ninety-five on 1 March 2020, was probably the most admired poet in Latin America after Pablo Neruda, though as personalities they could not have been more different. Lacking Neruda's charisma, Cardenal deployed a modest and thoughtful gentleness, which belied his administrative skills and his profoundly stubborn personality.

Born in Granada, Nicaragua in 1925, Cardenal studied literature in Mexico and the United States, where he developed a strong interest in the poetry of Ezra Pound: later in life he would repeatedly tell interviewers that Pound was his most important influence; indeed, 'for me the most important poet in the world'. Returning to Nicaragua in 1950, he joined the group of modernist writers known as *Generacion de 1940*, who rejected the elaborate rhetoric Nicaraguan poetry had inherited from Rubén Darío, as well as symbolist notions of *poésie pure*. Accordingly, much of his earliest poetry (collected in *Oraciones*, 1960) is public and political, even oratorical, in tone. Increasingly as time went on Cardenal came to incorporate historical documents, advertising copy, anthropological reports and other documents in his longer poems, very much on a Poundian model; though he was also adept at witty and bitter love lyrics with strong European influences (*Epigramas*, 1961). In 1954, implicated in a failed *coup* against the dictator Anasatazio Somoza, Cardenal fled the country and entered the Trappist monastery at Gethsemani, Kentucky. One fruit of his time at Gethsemani was a superb sequence of lyrics on subjects as various as the cicadas in the monastery garden, the incessant sound of traffic on the highway outside the gates, and the fates of friends tortured and executed by the Somoza régime.

Returning to Nicaragua in 1965, Cardenal was ordained priest and, tolerated at first by the government, founded a quasi-monastic community on Mancarrón, one of the Solentiname Islands in Nicaragua's largest lake. Attracting artists and writers, the colony became a centre of folk art, but it was also Cardenal's parish. He arranged readings from the New Testament after Sunday mass, inviting local subsistence farmers and fishermen to interpret the verses. Their responses supplied the substance of *The Gospel in Solentiname* (*El Evangelio en Solentiname*, 1975–77), a commentary on the Gospels which became a classic of liberation theology. In 1977, however, in response to local unrest the colony was attacked and burned by government troops and Cardenal fled to Costa Rica. Two years later the Somoza government was overthrown by the left-wing Sandinistas, who invited Cardenal to become Minister of Culture. His role as part of a revolutionary government was viewed badly in Rome: Pope John Paul II prohibited Cardenal from administering the sacraments. When the Pope visited Nicaragua, Cardenal's behaviour was characteristic: he knelt on the tarmac at Managua airport to accept his rebuke, and refused to relinquish his post. It was the current Pope, Francis, who removed the ban in 2019. Meanwhile history had moved on; Cardenal had found Ortega's Sandinista government too authoritarian and left the party, which itself lost power in 1990 in a country profoundly weakened by conflict with the US-funded 'Contras'.

Cardenal's later poetry concentrates especially on indigenous themes, attempting to translate and present with respect traditions and worldviews buried or marginalised by the dominant culture. *Los ovnis de oro* (*Golden UFOs*) includes 'El secreto de Machu Picchu', which draws on both Pound and Neruda to present the worldview, including the calendar, of the Inca civilisation displaced by the Spanish invaders, and depicts the Inca civilisation persisting, hidden within contemporary society and perhaps awaiting its time to re-emerge. Time, indeed, is cyclical and (in a way) spatial. Inverting William Gibson's aphorism about the future, one could say that for Cardenal – and, in his view, for the poor – 'the past is still here; it's just not evenly distributed'.

Cardenal remained a controversial figure: in old age, through death, and beyond. Although the dedication of the 2013 Poetry Festival in his honour signalled a certain consensus that he was now a recognised Nicaraguan hero, some sponsors (including at least one bank) withdrew their support. When he mounted the platform for his evening reading in Granada's central square, there were hoarse cries of '¡Viva Sandino!' from the back of the crowd, though whether in support or opposition was not clear. His funeral last month was disrupted by a small group of noisy Ortega supporters.

I met Cardenal as I browsed the bookstalls on the day after his reading, and told him how much I admired his work. We chatted amiably for a few minutes (Cardenal was virtually bilingual between English and Spanish) but no profundities were exchanged. He seemed tired; I didn't wish to impose. It was before the days of selfies, but a man in a suit (Cardenal's minder?) appeared as if from nowhere, seeming to assume that my main object was to be photographed with Cardenal. It hadn't even occurred to me; but I had a camera and meekly handed it over, so I have the pictures. It was an oddly unimpressive encounter, and, on reflection, typical of Cardenal. Like the indigenous people in his poems, he went his own way, quietly and stubbornly, remaining a touch enigmatic. The drama, wit and eloquence are in his poems, which are hardly known in the anglophone world and deserve much better.

Ernesto Cardenal and Sir Francis Drake

RICHARD GWYN

To schoolchildren of my generation, Sir Francis Drake was a hero, the epitome of English sangfroid, insisting on finishing his game of bowls before dealing with the Spanish Armada, as it sailed up the Channel. It didn't happen quite like that, of course, but who cares. The sea captains who forged the first imprint of Empire under Elizabeth I have gone down here as great patriots, but children in schools throughout Iberia and Latin America know them simply as pirates. I remember looking through the history homework of my friend Nelson Pereira's younger sister, Elsa, while staying at their house outside Lisbon in 1983 and being shocked to see Drake being vilified in categorical terms. I imagine he doesn't get much of a press in Irish school history books either, as he was involved in a massacre of 600 people during the English enforced plantation of Ulster in 1575. But that is how it goes: history is an imprecise art. Rather like fiction, in fact.

While in Argentina recently I got into a lengthy discussion about the pirate Drake, and buccaneers of his ilk, on discovering that Drake also entered the River Plate on his travels and sailed up the Paraná. I said to my companions that in Britain we did not speak of Drake as a pirate at all, not by any means, and that the first time I had heard him referred to in those terms was reading Gabriel Garcia Márquez's *One Hundred Years of Solitude*.

Following the death on 1 March of the great Nicaraguan poet Ernesto Cardenal – Rebel Priest, Sandinista, theologian, follower and friend of Thomas Merton, and translator of Ezra Pound – I started looking again at some of the lesser-known historical poems by Cardenal, and was struck by the Poundian flavour of some of these. I have always been particularly taken by the following poem, written in the voice of a Spanish sea captain and based on a true account, in which Drake comes across as quite honourable, in spite of his reputation among the Spanish as a fierce and terrible pirate.

DRAKE IN THE SOUTH SEA
Realejo, 16 April 1579
For Rafael Heliodoro Valle

I set out from the port of Acapulco on the twenty-third
   of March
and steered a steady course until the fourth of April, a
   Saturday,
and half an hour before daybreak
we saw a ship draw alongside us
its sails and prow silver in the moonlight
and our helmsman shouted at them to make way
and they might as well have been sleeping, for they did
   not reply.
Another voice shouted over: FROM WHERE DOES
   YOUR SHIP SAIL?
and they answered, from Peru, and that it was
   the *Miguel Angel*
and then we heard trumpets and the firing of muskets

and they ordered me to board their boat
and I was taken to the Captain.
I found him pacing on the bridge
and I approached him and kissed his hands, and he
   said to me:
What gold or silver does your ship carry?
And I told him: None at all.
None, my lord, only my plates and cups.
After which he asked me if I knew the Viceroy,
and I told him that I did. And I asked the Captain
if he was truly Captain Drake,
and he said he was, the very same.
We stayed talking a long while, until it was time to eat
and he ordered me to sit at his side.
His plates and cups are silver, with golden borders,
adorned with his coat of arms.
He has many bottled perfumes and scented waters
which he says were given him by the Queen.
He always eats and drinks to the accompaniment of
   violins,
and takes with him painters who make pictures all
   along the coast.
He is a man of some twenty-four years, small, with a
   blonde beard,
He is a nephew of the pirate Juan Aquinas,
and he is one of the greatest sailors on the seas.
The following day, which was a Sunday, he dressed in
   great style,
And ordered his men to hoist banners
and pennants of many colours at the mastheads.
The bronze rings and chains and embellished
   handrails
and the lights of the quarterdeck
shone like gold.
The ship was a golden dragon among the dolphins.
And we went, with his page, to my ship, to see the
   coffers,
and he spent the whole day, until nightfall, inspecting
   my cargo.
What he took from me was not much,
a few baubles I owned,
and he gave me a cutlass and a small silver brazier for
   them
asking my forgiveness,
but that it was for his lady he had taken them,
and I was free to leave in the morning as soon as there
   was a breeze
and I thanked him for that,
and kissed his hands.
He carries in his galleon three thousand bars of silver
and three coffers filled with gold
and twelve great coffers of pieces of eight,
and he says they are heading for China
with navigation charts and a Chinese pilot they
   captured...

Translated from the Spanish by Richard Gwyn

Down on the Farm

LUCY CHESELDINE

Life on a farm doesn't always mean living by one. When I arrived to work on a one-woman holding in Alabama, first things first, we lunched at an all-you-can eat Chinese on the nearest strip mall. We spent most of our time building a wire fence to keep trucks from veering onto the field full of medicinal herbs, while drivers in those same trucks honked at our bare legs. Fast forward four years and I'm on my way to another farm where life and work weren't always on a neatly mythic parallel: Donald Hall's ancestral home at Eagle Pond. His eventual settling there with poet Jane Kenyon, after years away at Harvard, Oxford, Stanford, and Michigan, was never as a farmer. In *A String Too Short to Be Saved*, he calls New Hampshire's agrarian world a 'perpetual elegy'. And, as the phrase suggests, it's one he's salvaged in language while remaining characteristically unsentimental about his remove from the soil. We live by our desires and some losses can't be recovered. But all these contradictions don't stop us from willing continuity. Nobody knew that as well as Don. Over a year after his death, the latest turn in Eagle Pond's history is starting to tell a similar story.

Hall died in the knowledge that his granddaughter would live at Eagle Pond, bringing in the new – technological, professional, ideal – while keeping the familial line. When that fell through, his family put the farm up for public sale. At that sale, last May, a group of intellectuals and academics banded together to buy the Wilmot plot and its contents. Plans are still vague but 'The Don and Jane Society' want to maintain the property as a museum and writers retreat. In one sense, this is the natural progression for a place that's steeped in linguistic succession. But it's not entirely cut and dried. By this move, we have to ask ourselves, do we risk making the farm a cultural object? Will it stand apart from its surroundings, or become another reminder of New England's fabled rural heritage? Most pressingly, will it meet the demands made of art in a shifting world? I want the farm to embrace its literary legacy. And I want to be a part of keeping it. But I think in practical management, we might seek to maintain Eagle Pond as a living and working place that reflects the need for diversity, inclusion, and outreach, remembering the changes Don made in the world outside the farm. And for that, his writing is our best guide. His was not a straightforward sense of an inheritance. What distinguishes him, I think, from his literary past, and what often gets left out of his perpetually elegiac reputation, are the sometimes subtle but always necessary embraces of change that belong to a life well lived.

Hall once wrote in a letter to Wendell Berry that 'Jane re-led me to the farm'; his later life cemented such re-bounds in his thinking by making homecoming an always present and shifting 'coming home to language'. The farm is a 'form', he tells us, with porous walls and open fields, which look onto future change. There's a moment in his poem 'Eating the Pig' when a cooked pig sits at the dinner table's centre. Looking at the carcass, the speaker's thoughts cross time, 'redoubling' their tracks like the dead creature's crisscrossed ribs. Imagining history condensed to single scene, he sits bereft before the pig, then:

> Without knowing that I will do it,
> I reach out and scratch his jaw,
> and I stroke him behind his ears,
> as if he might suddenly purr from his cooked head.

I've always found this moment one of the strangest in Hall's poetry. Perhaps because its disturbance ends in profundity. Everyone is outside of knowledge: the dead pig, the bemused speaker, the baffled reader. The poet, to some extent of course, knows what he's doing. But it's the not knowing that's important. It's the searching for something by entering time's flow. That, the lines tell us, is where love begins, in purring affection, and so too does poetry. Those of us who experience the history and future of Eagle Pond might well take these lines as a starting point: what we know is gone and what we can is unknown, and to reach the space in between, the space of language and conflict, we must learn to exist uncertainly between both. By this, we might do more than come home to language; we might extend that home into new ones.

Rush and Rand

WILLIAM POULOS

Neal Peart died in January. He was the drummer and lyricist for the progressive rock band Rush. The word 'progressive' here has nothing to do with politics: it describes a band with the energy and volume of rock music, but whose songs are often long and made of unusual structures and odd time signatures. Usual rock lyrics wouldn't suit songs like these: a caricature of a progressive rock band depicts the singer reciting *Lord of the Rings* over a solo harpsichord. Most prog rock bands aren't so – how else can I put it? – uncool, but don't sing about drinking beer or touching women's legs or driving fast cars.

Peart actually did write a song about driving a fast car, *Red Barchetta*, but it's based on Richard S. Foster's futuristic short story in which cars can withstand heavy impacts without hurting the driver. (In the song, the narrator has an old and now-illegal barchetta – a two-seater without a roof – that he drives every Sunday morning. One joyride turns into a chase as he flees two drivers in newer, safer cars trying to ram him.) Peart – affectionate-

ly known as 'The Professor' – was more bookish than most lyricists, and the lyrics for the twenty-minute-long song '2112' (on the album of the same name) are based on Ayn Rand's novella *Anthem*. Peart dedicated the song to 'the genius of Ayn Rand' and more impressive than his drumming ability was his ability to revive an interest in Ayn Rand's ideas and writing – something no one else could do, not even Ayn Rand.

So you could describe Rush as progressive in music and individualistic in politics. Even one of these attitudes is enough to destroy a career, but this combination made Rush one of the most popular progressive rock bands around. Their musicianship and songwriting – especially on the albums they released from the mid '70s to the early '80s – show that a band can have complex, intricate songs and still rock. Rush defies expectations: the modern American libertarian movement, which usually doesn't get excited about anything except tax-cuts and free trade, is excited about Rush.

Maybe the libertarians are drawn to Rush's music because of its unusual structures and mixed metres: a musical style appealing to their sense of individuality and eschewal of tradition. (If this were true, you'd think that they would be supporters of free-form jazz, but I suppose even libertarians have standards.) Since they aren't so enthusiastic about other prog bands such as Genesis and Pink Floyd, I imagine Rush appeals to them because of Peart's Randian lyrics. (Curiously, while Rand was alive her admirers were smarmy, almost cultic. In other words, they were groupies.) In a notorious interview with *NME*, Peart, echoing Rand, said that he thought productive work was the centre of man's life. The interviewer, Barry Miles, thought that this sounded too much like the gates of Auschwitz and compared the band to Nazis – a spectacularly stupid comment, considering that Rush's singer and bassist Geddy Lee descends from death-camp survivors.

Miles might have listened to the lyrics to better understand what Peart thinks about society and politics. The song '2112' itself describes The City of Megadon, a Temple of Syrinx, and a Solar Federation – a sci-fi dystopia too complicated for a rock tune. (I have sung and danced along with the lyrics 'we are the priests of the Temples of Syrinx' hundreds of times without ever knowing or caring what they actually meant.) The listener might twig the political significance only when the Priests of Syrinx proclaim: 'Hold the Red Star proudly.' The Priests represent a collectivist mindset, and Rush's logo depicts a man (i.e. the individual) resisting a (not always red) star.

Rush's other songs express similar political ideas without the sci-fi dressing. The second song on the album *2112* is 'A Passage to Bangkok', an ode to weed – a favourite libertarian vice – which is much blander than the title track. (I don't think this is a coincidence). The last song on the album is 'Something For Nothing' which has the lyrics: 'you don't get something for nothing / you don't get freedom for free... what you do is your own kingdom / what you do is your own glory.' This affirmation of personal responsibility sounds like a musical form of Ayn Rand's conception of 'man as a heroic being, with his own

happiness as the moral purpose of his life, with productive achievement as his noblest activity, and reason as his only absolute'. Rand thought that, in the absence of special bonds created by love or contract, we have no obligation to others' needs. Although she was known as a defender of 'selfishness' and *laissez-faire* capitalism, Rand was extremely generous to people in her personal life (including strangers) and tirelessly defended justice and the idea that people are ends themselves.

Rush's lyrics also provide more nuance than a textbook defence of *laissez-faire* capitalism. Peart was in his twenties when he wrote the lyrics for *2112* and as he aged his lyrics became more astute. In songs written in the mid-to-late '80s he criticized superficial materialism ('big money got a mean streak / big money got no soul') and the environmental destruction it causes ('rain is burning on the forest floor...sky full of poison / and the atmosphere's too thin'). These songs aren't well-known because they're musically limp compared to Rush's earlier work, raising an important question about how aesthetics and meaning interact. Songs are possibly the only form of art in which the aesthetic and semantic value aren't necessarily connected: many of Verdi's arias remain popular even though the libretto and the melody don't match. This ends up being difficult for those who perform to make a living. Some singers must play popular songs that no longer represent themselves or their views; they find their audience loves a person who no longer exists, a person in an old photograph they must imitate to keep selling tickets. Most prog rock bands prevent this problem early and write about topics that will remain popular (or unpopular) throughout their careers. Your lover might leave you, your political views might change, your fast car might be replaced by another vehicle, but *Lord of the Rings* will always be there to provide you with lyrics.

Letter from Wales

SAM ADAMS

That wonderfully informative series of chunky books, *The Buildings of Wales*, was founded by Sir Nikolaus Pevsner as an extension of his *Buildings of England*, but he was not their author. The much praised volume on Glamorgan was written by John Newman (who, while a student at the Courtauld, was for a time Pevsner's driver), and it is he who made the bold assertion that 'in Cathays Park, Cardiff has the finest civic centre in the British Isles ... where the coherence and splendour of the whole group (of buildings) adds lustre to each individual element'. Most of us, residents in or frequent visitors to Cardiff, are so accustomed to the neat assemblage of a dozen listed, mostly Edwardian baroque, buildings in pale Portland stone on a roughly rectangular grid, with the fine open space of Alexandra Gardens in the midst, that we rarely pause to take it in. It is a pleasant place to stroll on a fine day. You can walk its perimeter roads in twenty minutes without undue haste, as I often did during lunch

hours when I worked in the fortress-like 'New Crown Building', clearly designed like the castles of Edward I to keep down the rebellious Welsh, which, since 1979, has closed off the northern end. That and a few more recent additions apart, Cardiff's civic centre is grand without being overbearing, in keeping with the domestic scale of much of the city, until recent years and the construction 'down town' of a cluster of multi-storey monstrosities that crowd the sky without offering a glimmer of aesthetic interest.

Just across the road from the civic centre, to the west, is Cardiff Castle, which has Roman and Norman origins and at the beginning of the fifteenth century fell to the greatest of Welsh rebels, Owain Glyndwr. The castle owes its present form to the ambition of successive marquesses of Bute and especially to the productive partnership of John Crichton-Stuart, third marquess, with the Victorian Gothic architect-designer, William Burges. The faux-medieval interior of the castle is one of the wonders of Wales and hardly matched anywhere else, though a runner-up might be Castell Coch, just six miles north, a fairy castle overlooking the Taff gorge that you glimpse as you pass by on the M4, which was rebuilt and decorated in similar style by the same partnership of patron and genius. The third marquess owned 22000 acres in the old county of Glamorgan alone, with its mineral rights, in the great years of coal. His gross income is reported to have been £300,000 per annum, roughly the equivalent of £37 million today. One of the richest men in the world at the time, if not the richest, he could afford Burges's architectural and decorative flights of fancy.

In 1898 the marquess sold 59 acres of what had been Cardiff castle's pleasure grounds for £161,000 to the local council and this was the land on which the civic centre gradually developed. Today the site has four Grade I listed buildings: City Hall and the Crown Court, both opened in 1906, what was formerly known as Glamorgan County Hall (1912), and the National Museum of Wales, on which work also began in 1912 but, because of delays occasioned by the First World War, opened in 1922. The eight Grade II listed buildings include Cardiff University's main building, the first stage of which was completed in 1909, and the Temple of Peace, a latecomer to the architectural ensemble and somewhat different in style, which opened in 1938. Strictly 'the Temple of Peace and Health', the latter was the gift of David Davies, 1st Baron Davies (grandson of his namesake, the great nineteenth century Welsh industrialist), who had fought in the First World War. His aim was to provide a memorial to those who had lost their lives in the conflict and a home for an organisation dedicated to the elimination of the scourge of tuberculosis. His sisters, Margaret and Gwendoline, who also went to war and served with the French Red Cross, in moments of release from their duties visited Paris in pursuit of art. Their bequests in 1951 and 1963 gave the National Museum, just a couple of hundred yards away, one of the world's finest collections of Impressionist and Post-Impressionist paintings.

The Temple of Peace, which can now be hired for events, has become the new home of Seren's Cardiff Poetry Festival, held this year across a weekend in mid-February. Festival director Amy Wack assembled a programme tailored to a wide range of interests including workshops and readings and a 'Desert Island Poems' session with singer-songwriter James Dean Bradfield, leader of that most literate and poetically aware group the Manic Street Preachers, interviewed by Meic's far-famed broadcasting son, Huw Stephens. Peter Finch, a prolific writer of psychogeography and poetry, read from his latest collection of poems, *The Machineries of Joy,* (2020), his thirteenth book from Seren. He is probably the finest living exponent of 'sound poetry' both on the page and, as it needs to be, crisply vocalised. The large audience was duly appreciative. Peter is consistently and richly inventive – and entertaining, but a sharply critical mind guides the ingenious playfulness with 'words... words', and a dark thread runs through this latest book in poems from a road trip to the states, and about old, dead, poet-friends to hospital experiences, carrying the insistent message of mutability. Friday evening brought the inaugural Meic Stephens Lecture, sponsored by the Rhys Davies Trust, on 'creative correspondences' in the poetry of John Ormond. Kieron Smith's timely reminder of his subject's rare talent as both poet and film-maker, was particularly apt, for *Poetry Wales*, launched by Meic Stephens in 1965, helped give John Ormond a reason to turn to poetry again, after early discouragement from Vernon Watkins. He used to say he wrote 'Cathedral Builders', a poem with which he will always be associated, in 'twenty minutes flat' and sent it off to the new magazine with 'Design for a Tomb', a fascinating mixture of the funereal and the subtly erotic. They appeared together in the summer 1966 number and he was once more in the groove. Re-reading his *Collected Poems* (Seren, 2015), which appeared twenty-five years after his death, edited by his daughter Rian Evans, reminds us of the range of his interests – in art and architecture, archaeology, music, philosophy, science and the natural world. All contributed to the rich veins of imagery that thread his poems. He also drew on the inspiration afforded by his home and his family, and by Tuscany, where he was a frequent visitor in his later years. The primary concerns of birth, love and death run through all his work. He found no answers to the fundamental questions, but as he sought them his poetry continued to develop and move along unexpected avenues of thought and feeling. Smith's lecture and his book John Ormond's *Organic Mosaic* (UWP 2019) remind us he is a genuinely significant poet.

From the Journals

R.F. LANGLEY

[continued from issue 252]
Gislingham church, Suffolk, 25 August 1974

The gallery built across the tower arch as a vestry, with three glass windows with nylon drapes, is Indian red, subdued, flat, unresonant beneath the windows. Then the rest ochre. Above that the plastered walls, everywhere flaked, bitted, the Naples yellow, white yellow, over whiter bared skin, scabbing wearing. Then the brown benches and the dark stained box pews, the muted bricks and tiles of the floor, every place running in different directions, sizes and shades, red tiles with vein-blue blotted centres. Raw red ones like lipstick where someone smothered rudding as for front steps and it soaked. Mostly age-pale beige bricks, yellowish. All toned and fractured and agglomerated together in a matrix holding all the possibilities in drawn breath. The cheap light brown of the three-decker pulpit, raw textured, no juice. The wine-red and blue carpet.

Then the intensifications catching up all this saturation. The old glass in small oblongs and circles in window edgings - violent clear orange, blue, green, jewelled points. Softer the figured glass - two kings, heads gone and replaced by frosted blanks, sit and face each other, raise a hand, argue, in pale blue robes with ermine collars. Blue columbine swirls, faded, on gold stems which sweep, or plait. A foot appears with big vigorous toes. A face, right at the bottom, shorn of hair, ear and all, vacuous.

Then the organ, pipes and upper casing painted battleship silver-grey, coarse but instantly catching up the slate in the big wall plaque to the Godbold Rainbirds, Elizabeth and John and dead young children who 'never sinned'. The organ case belted with a cord of gold and royal blue twists. The royal blue of the short curtain frill hung on the rail on the pews level with the doors, of the pulpit cloths. Clear as deep sky. And fouled by droppings, already old.

The Bedingfield monument in the chancel painted hard and yet not quite venomous - he in matt black, his fine meaty folding cloth and gunbelt of rolled tucks sling off his shoulder. His hair paintbox-yellow-brown, his face and hands flour-white, and yellow-green kerchief draped over the skull. All repressed colours, all unjustified and, probably, ruination on a good monument (undated but the pillars are black touch, white capitals - Stone time, 1615? *) but this morning they speak out and the eye moves off finding the same notes.

The diamond panes in windows have been partly replaced by clear glass so that one doubts there is glass at all in these random patches. Quilted hotch potch like the floor.

Outside iceclouds pile across and sweep by. The nettles and burnt grass and blackened umbellifers are deep. The sills are below their heads. Looking out, the long hulk of the church is low in the water. Mountain ash thrash, elders, some sort of shining-leaved laurel gone wild. Meadow cranesbill bleaches white against the footings.

Through the back south window air comes. A hole. And the light in a crockery shade creaks on its long chain. A blue tit climbs on it. Best of all a spotted flycatcher is in the roof, with a nest in an oak hole at the base of the second hammerbeam, back on the south of the nave. The bleached, hacked wood warps apart. Dark ground of timbers with newer, browner, shinier replaced boards above in the interstices. Web threads hang weighted with bits and flakes. A burr of wings. The neatness. The worried tail, wet-white chin and throat, pale eye-stripe, more chestnut back, dark big eye and maybe lavender-mauve, some plum-like hue misted over the whole from scarce-seen striations on the chest. The path from the rear window, along the middle air, time for three bursts of wings. Then arrival on a rusted metal rod across the roof. From there to the top of the embattled hammerbeam, walking there, cocking and peering, and cheeping confidentially,

watching us for a long time before dropping down into the knotted hole where the profile of his head bobs, feeding, beakfuls of crane-flies, a grub, very quickly, then back.

The battlements repercuss, ranges of them on the cornice of the roof, on the double layer of hammers, in each window as the three-part stepped transom effect in the head. In these cities the bird hurries. Blues and browns, creams and reds, refine, fine out in his live shift. A white mute is dropped.

The chancel corbel figures, knob-eyed men holding shields, scrolls and musical instruments glower. One proud. Another cynical, trenched sneer and thick lips, deep-socketed eyes and hunched around a big rough lute, stubbed hands grip and bang. Rubbish hangs on them in strings, badges of birdlime in small shot bursts, furred lines of web, spinning flakes of plaster. They scowl. Hands have been smashed off, they are chopped, clawed, split and filthy.

The font's beasts are smooth iron clamps. The iron hook behind the door, a heavy metal staff, pivots on a thick metal ring sunk into the plaster so that the solid bar grates, grinds out of fixity in matrix.

The thousand tints are pocked, rain-blurred, mossed, rubbed, peppered with worm like the white-shocked dried-out benches or the loose-boarded floor under them, yet held in this fixity of vast proportions.

The foundered ark. Long body, capacious windows, wide wall spaces, massive rust-red tower turreted at each corner - colours take off, brick vertical-prowed ashlar-grey. A thick taste of rusty iron, slate, cool on the tongue, cream plaster, curded flaking, clean penetrating drops of lime, of sulphur, stirred milk of pale brick, tables of grave sweets, garnished, massive ingestion.

The cold powerful key, finger-thick, clinks in the lock. The heavy door judders back, colours leap up and scatter and then stand ranged around, piled, matched and interlocked.

Pied wagtails fly up under dark avenues of trees. An age-grey slipper rippling fur of a running squirrel's tail. Skeins of crows. Blank Woolpit brick fringed with calamint sweet pink or herb Robert's purpling leaves. A drift of blue-grey umbellifers, small and dry, in Redgrave churchyard. Blue velvet, pure mutes, earth coming through dust, the finished and over, at its splendid ranked great celebration held asunder together in a keeling hulk rolling in weeds unsunk, castellated lions on the door with wide almond eyes, and thonged tails tipped in whips of thick fire, crusted with growths; substances intensify, go themselves then vanish leaving colours in the water of the air which cannot be undone. Priceless trash. Brilliant bungling.

Back at five we sit in the car as the cloudburst comes at last, banging the lid with rolls of hail, pouring water under the back door, the wind forcing it through.

* *RFL refers to the sculptor Nicholas Stone*

(Edited by Barbara Langley, April 2020)

On the Surface of Events

Rereading the Book of Jonah

Iain Bamforth

WHEN I WAS SMALL and Biblical and made to realise that my Brethren parents saw no nuance in the matter of salvation – either you were swallowed whole by giant belief or spat out among the unsaved – I was irresistibly drawn to the story of Jonah's going down to the lower deck of the ship taking him from Joppa to Tarshish. He is trying to reach the latter place, which present-day historians believe to have been the city of Carthage or a port on a trading island in the western Mediterranean, perhaps Sardinia, in order to avoid the divine command to get up and go to the glittering capital of the Assyrian empire, Nineveh – 'that great city, and cry against it'. Nineveh lay overland, in the opposite direction altogether.

Like Adam in the Garden of Eden, Jonah is trying to hide from his maker.

Even as the wind starts to torment the haunted waters of the eastern Mediterranean, Jonah, who must have known that fish were more likely to climb trees than he ever get to Tarshish, decides to steal a quick nap in order to prepare himself for the possibly sterner trials ahead. Jonah goes to his sleeping quarters during what turns out to be an almighty bluster called up by the same Divine One, a squall so sudden and fierce even the ship itself has terrible visions, as the Hebrew original says: it thinks it's going to capsize. This little ship would have much preferred to stay in a harbour.

Going below deck in the middle of a tempest for a snooze is an egregious act; being able to sleep through the chaos and commotion of an impending maritime disaster marks Jonah out as much odder still. The Hebrew keeps hinting that his 'going down' is a descent from conventional experience into something far more abyssal.

The only paying passenger makes himself conspicuous by making himself scarce: a precondition for surviving really bad storms is a collective effort to ride them out – 'all must contribute their Quota of Exertion', according to Coleridge (who had a bit of experience with storms in the Mediterranean). If a ship is anthropomorphic, and this roiling sea a formless argument of (as we shall discover) higher-sphere attributions, then all hands are needed on deck. Indeed, the sailors are already bailing out the hold and heaving everything overboard – their Bronze Age goods along with the contents of their stomachs. Every single bit of extraneous ballast has been thrown to the waves. And Jonah sleeps on, in a stupor or trance, insensible to the tumult thundering around him. Either he's shamming dead, or trying to pass himself off as a philosopher.

That great precursor of the modern novel François Rabelais wrote a similar scene into *Gargantua and Pantagruel.* When Panurge encounters a storm at sea, in the Fourth Book, Rabelais leaves us in no doubt that his heroes wish they had been elsewhere too: 'Believe me, it seem'd to us a lively Image of the Chaos, where Fire, Air, Sea, Land, and all the Elements, were in a refractory Confusion' (in Sir Thomas Urquhart's translation). In their distress, Panurge and Pantagruel eventually call out for the assistance of all the blessed saints. On Jonah's boat, the sailors have evidently made similar if more animistic assumptions. One: a raging sea and fierce winds can only correlate to the anger of a god. Two: if they make a great show of throwing material objects overboard, they may be able to assuage this god's wrath. Three: but whose god is it that's in a huff? Nobody knows. These sailors are a rum bunch, since every man is appealing, as the verse says, 'unto his god'.

Anthropologically speaking, this is how humans respond to a gathering menace: we cut peripheral losses in order to stave off the looming core catastrophe. In moments of crisis, we try to make ourselves lighter. To rid ourselves of ballast.

The entire cargo has gone, but it doesn't calm the sea. The helmsman wakes Jonah, and urges him to 'call upon' his god, like the rest of the crew, in order to avert disaster. In the very next moment – in that abruptly foreshortened way the Bible has of moving on the action – lots are being drawn (in what seems an attempt to divine the intentions of that blind goddess later known to the Romans as Fortuna) and Jonah is owning up to being a Hebrew, somebody who, for all his disregard for the fate of others, is actually in awe of Yahweh, the Lord God of the heavens, 'which hath made the sea and the dry land'. His admission certainly puts the wind up the rest of the men on board, because they now know that they are implicated in a bigger storm: one that has everything to do with Jonah's being on their ship.

Terrified, the sailors try to row the ship towards land, and make no progress. Oars have never been much use in a storm. The men can't swim either – but who among sailors has ever taken swimming lessons? In this regression into total helplessness that is the mark of every emergency Jonah does the right thing: he *volunteers* to leave the storm-tossed ship: he knows he's the true cause of this commotion. He has the courage to be thrown overboard although he lacked it to go to Nineveh. 'So they took up Jonah, and cast him forth into the sea: and the sea ceased from her raging.' Man overboard does the trick. The sea calms, and the crew – being now 'exceedingly fearful' of Jehovah – decide to offer up another sacrifice in their overwhelming gratitude to the Hebrew God. The nature of this offering is unspecified: there can't have been much left on board. Perhaps it was Jonah's luggage.

Out of sight, Jonah, as every child used to know, has been swallowed by a sea monster 'prepared' by the Almighty. This is both an act of mercy and a punishment. It is a delayed response – a kind of dream supplement – to his earlier attempt to find a moment of rest as the storm assailed the ship.

The philosopher Gaston Bachelard called this act of

bodily assimilation 'the Jonas complex', and observed that the notion of the 'eater eaten' (and yet surviving the act of bodily incorporation) is a common theme in children's stories. Phantasies of eating and being eaten are related to curiosity about the big questions of whence we come and whither we go. Jonas gets to spend three days knocking about in a great fish, the smelly insides of which must have resembled the rounded hull of another boat – a Phoenician cargo ship perhaps, ribbed just like those famous caravels Niña, Pinta or Santa Maria many, many centuries later. He has been removed from the belly of a ship to that of a great fish, and it is so dank and imposing that Jonah calls it Sheol: he is in the belly of hell. Lost to the world, condemned to his own company, he addresses God with a plaintive psalm in which he can see 'the bars of the earth closing upon [him] for ever'. He asks to be delivered from this tenemented refuge. He has seen the dark inside of events, and he wants out.

And God has the fish vomit Jonah up on dry land.

When word comes again from the Almighty to go to Nineveh and tell its inhabitants that the city has forty days before it gets wiped off the map, Jonah drops everything and goes. Now the private person and the public office are one. A prophet has no ego, a prophet can't withhold, a prophet doesn't argue: he's simply announces what he's told to say. He's a *loudspeaker*. When he gets to Nineveh – a kind of sea monster done up as a city – he discovers it is such a grand place that it takes three days to walk from the west gate to the east gate, as tallied by the punctilious Sir Thomas Browne: 'So that if Jonah entered at the narrower side, he found enough for one Daye's walk to attain the heart of the City, to make his Proclamation.' Jonah cries against the citizens, crying in the Bible being sometimes less an act of communication than a hoarse exultation – God is vexed! Just wait and see what's coming your way!

What happens is something altogether unheralded: the people of Nineveh listen to his message. They hearken, as the Bible says, to the five prophetic words. Like the sailors in the boat to Tarshish, the people of Nineveh are susceptible to Jonah's words. '[A]ll genuine Morality, all applied practical vivified Moral Eloquence, is essentially prophetic', wrote Coleridge. The whole city of Nineveh – under orders from the king – dons sackcloth and ashes, even the livestock is smeared with the stuff; and as Jonah walks through the streets he can hear the citizens 'crying mightily' to God. This is not the same kind of crying as was heard earlier from his throat: this is something that spills out of people's mouth and resembles the phenomenon Socrates calls 'opinion' in Plato's *Philebus*. Opinion is public and fearful; it can't be held in and it won't tolerate dissent.

The act of public penance works. When God hears the prayers of the people of Nineveh, he decides not to carry out his promise to level the city. 'And God repented of the evil that He had said that He would do unto them; and He did it not.'

Jonah understands that he has been made to look ridiculous. His vision has taken in water, lots of it, and sunk ignominiously – to revert to the imagery of his earlier adventure. And by the agency of none other than the one true God, who is in one of his less readable moods.

So all that business with the storm and sea monster was just a kind of joke! He even confesses to Jehovah that he suspected this might happen all along, which is why he had tried to escape to Tarshish in the first instance! A disturbing question takes shape in the mind, ours as was as his. What kind of prophet can he be if the weight of his world-historical warning is annulled simply by people acting upon its threat? That makes his prediction something less than a first-order truth. A prophecy and its fulfilment – aren't those two sides of an event that has no front or back, no right or left, which is the same truth however perceived? As George Steiner points out, a prophet's use of the future tense is 'merely tautological'.

Perhaps Jonah isn't a prophet at all but that modern thing: a *weather-forecaster*. But what on earth was he predicting? Did he even know? 'The expert is a man who has stopped thinking – he knows!', the architect Frank Lloyd Wright is reported to have said. Experts get it right but sometimes they get it wrong, and wildly wrong at that. It even appears as if the king of Nineveh – sitting in cinders, with all his advisors around him wearing grey – might even possess more insight into God's intentions that his appointed prophet. And Jonah can hardly fail to have noticed that the Almighty himself is in flagrant contradiction of the law of direct reciprocal justice. Nineveh had been wicked enough to bring itself to His attention – and here it is, still glittering and splendid, its towers and flagstones intact, and all its debts cancelled. Surely the message from an angry God didn't come with a non-performance clause?

This dramatic change in Nineveh's fortunes so riles Jonah that he goes into a deep sulk. He camps outside the city walls. By merely hanging around he means to force Jehovah to wipe it off the map. (Rembrandt made a sketch of the scene in 1655.) Imagine! God commands him to proclaim the religion of impending doom – and then the doom doesn't happen! All his brother prophets, too, had vowed Nineveh would become 'a desolation'. To be prophetic was to show how the great scroll of universal history unfolded from the Word, as the Book of Deuteronomy says – anything else was merely human conceit. 'When a prophet speaks in the name of the Lord, if the thing follow not, nor come to pass, that is the thing which the Lord has not spoken; the prophet has spoken it presumptuously; be not afraid of him.' Prophecy is a rebuke, as well as a declaration of things to come. Prophecy is as irreversible as time itself. How could he, Jonah, be wrong on such a key issue?

Jonah is exhibiting, as Elias Canetti writes, 'the most repulsive and dangerous trait in a prophet': having foretold the most terrible events he *needs* them to come true. As we now know, being a prophet has nothing to do with the private life: being a prophet is to exercise a public function. Any dark glamour the calling has comes from being able to say 'I told you so' – but in the name of the Lord. Someone might have written in the Talmud that whoever saves a life saves the world, but at this moment in time Jonah doesn't give a jot about other lives. He just doesn't want to be remembered as a phoney.

God asks Jonah if he is right to get angry at what hasn't happened. He seems to be trying to win Jonah round to the viewpoint that he, the Lord of all Creation, is an artist: somebody who doesn't have to believe what he is capable of doing, but merely has to entertain it as a *possibility*. (Had Jonah suspected this, he could have reminded the Lord of all Creation that a religion without prophets is bound, in the fullness of time, to subside into a cult of universal happiness.)

Observing Jonah's discomfort as he sits sulking outside the city walls, at risk of sunstroke, God causes a miraculous gourd to spring up beside him in order to protect him from the heat and glare: Jonah isn't unappreciative of its shelter. This plant grows fast, miraculously fast. 'It grew faster than any plant outside Eden, by sinuous thrusts, putting out leaves like geese stretching their wings', as Guy Davenport has it, in his adaptation of the story. But the next day God withers the gourd: as straightforward a procedure as flattening a city. Now the desert wind blowing in from the east is so stifling it causes Jonah to faint from the oppressive heat. When he comes round he is even angrier: he tells Jehovah that he is going to be in a funk 'even unto death'. He wants to die not only because of his physical torment; he is in 'ideological' distress too, as Jonathan Magonet puts it. Such is the pride of prophets. God continues to reason with him, drawing an *a fortiori* argument out of Jonah's chagrin about the here-today gone-tomorrow gourd – 'which came up in a night, and perished in a night' – and the rather more considerable matter of the fate of the city of Nineveh: 'And should not I spare Nineveh, that great city, wherein are more than sixscore thousand [a formulaic Biblical number indicating *very many*] persons that cannot discern between their right hand and their left hand; and also much cattle?'

The Everlasting is scoring rhetorical – and ethical – points off his prophet.

The critic Harold Bloom insists that the four chapters of Jonah constitute the drollest, most 'Swiftian' book in the Tanakh. He also wonders whether the compilers of the canon dumped the Book of Jonah among the other minor prophets (Hosea, Joel, Amos, Obadiah, Micah, Nahum, Habakkuk, Zephaniah, Haggai, Zechariah, Malachi, all of whose names I was once able to recite in correct order of presentation to my parents) in order to conceal its sublime subversive farce. After all, the chronicler has just exposed the petulant Jonah as a false prophet, and cast doubt on the very efficacy of prophecy itself. Future prophets are going to have to bring glad tidings, at least as an optional extra.

The chronicler of the Book of Jonah certainly raises some incongruities. After his initial recalcitrance, Jonah is ultimately shown to take the whole business of a summons from the future more seriously than God himself. Having initially been presented as a rather sympathetic shirker who wanted to have nothing to do with the dubious glamour of being a prophet, he ends up embodying the very evil he threatens people with. Jonah, as that distinguished reader and writer Jorge Luis Borges might have said, finds himself trapped in the labyrinth ordinary beings call *time*. What we say about the future influences how it turns out: that is one of the folds peculiar to this labyrinth. We could even say that future events happen because we all have a universally shared conception of what the future *is*. In that sense, the future is a fixed point in the present.

The chronicler further reveals a Jehovah who, to convince Jonah of his powers, withers a pumpkin. (Jerome is his translation indicates that the Hebrew word *qiqayon* translated in the Septuagint as 'gourd' actually refers to a kind of preternaturally rapid-growing, self-supporting plant 'having large leaves like a vine', something like the magically sprouting seed in the story of Jack and the Beanstalk; Everett Fox in his new translation of the book identifies it – following Henri Meschonnic – as 'a castor-oil plant'). The comedy of the scene is lost on Jonah. If displaying mercy means eliminating not the wrongdoing – an impossibility in any case – but rather the resentment that follows a wrong we never get to find out whether Jonah ultimately acquires generosity and fellow-feeling. That would require him to recover some of the insouciance he showed at the tale's beginning.

So where the Book of Job ends with the unjustly suffering Job silent in adoration, the Book of Jonah ends with Jonah mired in perplexity.

It has been said that there is no humour in the Bible. Humour doesn't necessarily come in guffaws. We are left to consider the scene, as Jehovah spells out his rationale for sparing the inhabitants of Nineveh: although humans can't tell their right hand from their left the city is also full of 'much cattle' which merit consideration. Cattle are dumb and don't talk back.

Uniquely among the books of the bible, the Book of Jonah ends with a question: it is the voice of God – Yahweh or Elohim, since both names are present in the Book of Jonah – asking why it should be impossible for Him to be moved by a charitable impulse towards the beings He has nurtured, especially if they lack common sense. It is an ending that teeters on ambivalence, in a book that is all about turnings: the Eternally Prescient Predictor has learned to feel pity, although only a moment before He might just as easily have wiped a city off the face of the earth. It suggests a future where divine prophecy will be able to walk away from its implications, even as Jonah, a little man at the last, petulantly insists on a more deterministic universe.

Once More the Sea

PHOEBE POWER

The beach is bipartite, in process, divided. Half is brown-grey sludge, a packed-in powder. We walk on its springy surface, which feels like earth. Several inches high, this caked-up layer slumps on the limestone rocks beneath. Its dust, over a century's industry, clogs the cracks and hiding-places, pores, spaces between stones, till breathing is constricted.

The other half of the beach is loose. Our feet jangle pebbles in a clattering and jumble of many colours: red-speckled, praline, blue merle, yellow, a piece of inky coal. I pocket it. Water tumbles around all of them and the stones rattle freely, shifting from place to place a wrack of seaweed, fragments of shell, part of a crab, a fingerbone of wood.

Dissolving the soft clump stuck on this shore, the sea calmly erases what has gone on here. The job is only halfway done, half-started. Year on year and inch by inch, as the ocean inexorably shakes the dust free, the whiter stone finds itself again, ghostly and exposed.

‎ ‎ ‎ ‎—

In the beginning, there was the Earth, and it had been for four billion years.

At this time there was a forest. Drenched, and crackling with zigzag ferns and sunburst leaves. Metre-wide dragonflies ruled the air, while millipedes, several feet long, eased between mossy towers.

Over millions and millions of years, the trees died and fell into the swamp. Instead of decomposing, they slipped deeper underground, piling up in layers of peat. As the material gradually sank further down, nearer to the furnace of Earth's centre, heat and pressure combined in a marvellous trick. The plants were cooked, carbonised hard black.

The carbon inhaled repeatedly by unthinkable multitudes of generations of leaves and fronds, moss-tails, wasn't breathed out by bacteria in the gradual way, so it stayed locked-in, frozen in time or set like a diamond, a dark eye flash, liable to explode.

‎ ‎ ‎ ‎—

But I see the sea once more, wrote the poet from his guest room, eyeing the grey January tides as they rubbed the limbs of Seaham, in 1815.

When I visit the town, I notice Byron's Place, a harbour-facing retail complex with Betfred, Greggs and Wilko. In the paved zone outside stands a wooden sculpture of Byron and his Seaham wife, Annabella. Their torsos are hard and stretched-looking, legs stiffly raised,

apparently dancing; carved eyes stare beyond each other. On the plinth, some choice quotations from B's best-loved works: *she walks in beauty…* lines not meant for her.

Lizzie put *Byron* on her Tinder profile and got a message back which said I love the burger chain too! There isn't one in Seaham, just a clean-eating café with vegan options, recently opened. Lizzie studied Maths; so did Annabella.

'Never liked a prude – dowdy – knows Statistics! – bad figure – long & a high dress – still, she gains by inspection – the lower part of her face is bad – knows Greek & Latin.' Her calmness, self-command, while he bullied her made him prickle, but

'ha! She is like a child, quite caressable, I had her on the sofa. One animal is as good as another, provided she is young. Took her out of Seaham (shudder) to Augusta's, proved I could do without her. Still, I worked them both well, and left her for Geneva.'

‎ ‎ ‎ ‎—

Leslie shows me her driftwood sculptures. Cupboards of them, under the bed and piled up in the garage. Village scenes and abstract arrangements; model boats with sails; a little bird. She uses the sea-shaped contours as she finds them, emphasising with a rusty lock nailed in, for example, or a stretch of net or wire. On the workbench is a jar of sea glass like blue opals, ready to fill in skies or windows, dot a creature's eye. I'm not allowed to collect any more! she says, not till I've got through this – heaps of scavenged pieces stowed in sacks, ready to be worked. Haven't got space for it all. But I can't stop!

‎ ‎ ‎ ‎—

Bob and Michael let me share their Thursday walk. The meadow's full of purple clover

Funny, walking for pleasure on
the ground we used to work under.
I liked the small spaces, close around me body.

Not me. I'm glad they closed the pits.
Those of us who saw it coming made a plan.
I retrained, became a teacher, Geography and SEN.

Miners know all sorts of useful things.
Some young person doesn't know what to do,
I'll teach them how to hang a door.

When I go to decorate a house, sometimes it's haunted.
You got it in the mines too, spots where folk had died.
Close by you felt a funny feeling, a coldness.

Are you a spiritual person? Bob asks. Me, I've been med-itating for years and reached nirvana a few times. Only thing is after you die, what's it called, recycl– reincarna-tion. I'm not sure about that. That's a grey area for me.

Bob's Leave, Michael's Remain. As soon as this is said I feel a wedge occur in our trio that wasn't there before. Normal-ly this isn't discussed on their regular walks; friends-since-primary-school talk cars and tools. But it'll be all right though, insists Bob. He recommends Pink Himalayan salt for cooking; it's purer, you can look it up online.

—

I wake to coal-dark skies, rain thrown against the light-house windows. A sudden summer storm, tropical typhoon. I force myself to leave the cottage and catch the bus to Sunderland, where I change for another. I get off beside a grey block with a sign in small letters: COM-MUNITY CENTRE.

Inside, kettle's on and there's movement, warmth: Fri-day's Get Online group. They'd like to video-call relatives, order online products, but it's a social group really.

The trouble with us, says Iris, is it goes in one – and out – ! And next week we've forgotten everything.

Patient Jacob demonstrates how to save a picture as. Not save link! Right or left? someone asks. The students sit up straight at their PCs, and give each other hints. At 11.00 it's time for another cup of tea.

—

Will's cross because some bikers have just lobbed stones and left dents above the windscreen of his Land Rover. They're not allowed to run their motorbikes along his coastal paths.
I'll take you to the village I grew up in, he says.
We go to one of the access points to the land he man-ages, a route down to the beach. It's popular with flytip-pers and today the Council are there with a crane, removing a dilapidated sofa from a mess of papers and wrappers. An aged interpretation sign declares it was fun at the beach at Horden! alongside photos of 20s bathers, striped and smiling.
From the clifftop we observe a luminescent, cobalt-vi-olet pool, elongated on the beach below. It contrasts mysteriously with the sky's azure and the muted grass-land that we're walking on, a toxic mirror leached from machinery abandoned underground. The high iron con-tent has dyed similar pools further up the coast a poi-sonous shade of orange. But no one seems to know exactly what it is. Will says they had a pH test done and got a score of +1, like battery acid. I used to drive my push-bike through those pools, he says, everyone did.
It's going to come back to bite us, he continues, what's down there. When I bought my house they said have you considered subsidence. No one's sure. They're going to build the station at Horden; in a few years the cliff could erode right up to the main line. Remember the 'Beast from the East'? The sea foam rose and filled this whole area; afterwards nothing looked the same. Another one of those, and who knows where we'll be.

We drive through streets. The best tattooist in the north-east is based here, he tells me.

—

As soon as I am folded in, I breathe out and relax. The forest suits dull weather, damp tinted green-and-grey, ringing my eyes with wakefulness.

At the base runs the burn, tucked beside wide, palm-shaped leaves. They might be wild rhubarb, but I don't always know the names. I just cross the dene-mouth briefly, following the coastal path.

On my way out, I pass a chorus of hello! orange flowers like strings of dripped jewels, their colour a deep lit eye. I will find their name later and they turn out to be *Montbretia*, an African species brought to English gardens in 1880. They'd escape to wildlands by 1911. And through

the arch of the towering
red-brick Viaduct,
I am back at sea. Brown butterflies
frisk my hair

—

We are making a banner for the parade. Grace has drawn it all out in black marker pen: the stripes of the rainbow, outlines of the boy and girl holding hands, and the name of the village in block capitals. Keep in the lines! she begs the others. The adults and helpers cut out squares of coloured felt with the big scissors, then the children take the pieces and coat them with PVA to stick on the banner. Ruby takes pleasure in painting the back of her hand with a thick layer, letting it dry then peeling off the rub-bery shape, holding it like a ghost before scrunching it away. Don't use up all the glue doing that, says Jodie. She's got two tattoos on her forearms. The goddess Isis and her daughter's name in sign language.
Are you coming to my den after this? asks Evie. It's got a working tap.
Will you come home with me I don't like walking in the numbered streets, says Grace.
I like reading, says Mark, with bright, fast eyes, *Diary of a Wimpy Kid* and *Goosebumps*. And I've got the Lion Witch and Wardrobe book. What do you want to do when you grow up? Play out. Kids these days, they're always on their phones. His dad takes him on long walks down the dene. Do you know the way to the beach? *We* do. Some mums don't bring the bairns on the trips, they don't actually like nature themselves, they find it boring.
Miss Mop, Miss Mop! Kian and Evie stand opposite each other, and clap:

x   x
Miss Mop.
x   x
Miss Mop.
x
Miss
x   x   x x x x
Mop from California,
x   x   x   x
Sitting on a bench, learning French

As the rhythm accelerates Kian wiggles his body with delight and Mark beside him, older brother not joining in directly, can't help his face from laughing too

```
x        x        x    x   x
Watching the clock go Tick, tock
   x  x    X
Tick tock Ban-a-na
```
____

Denise provides us each with a fluorescent jacket like builders wear, and a picker, complete with claw. Snap snap: children love them. Connor tells me he's sharing the grabber with his brother.

   Ian's semi-retired and looking for opportunities
     to meet people

   Staff from a health food chain are fundraising
     for a dog charity

   Julie loves to paint the sea
     but it's so difficult

It already looks clean: most of the bits are small, scraps tucked between stones or tied into seaweed, torn like driftwood. Wire, glass, metal, lots of discoloured sea-washed plastic of all types, the colours of the pebbles. You don't see it till you look.
____

I used to live in the mountains, says the owner of the cafe,

   das war meine Heimat
   aber ich mag die Küste...
____

I continue along the beach, which is gradually changing colour: from dark-brown to tan, then golden. I wade through piles of light, fine sand springing tufts of grass, and the wind passes over its hand and leaves an uneven, wrinkled pattern.

I stand in the sea. Wellbeing spreads from my toes to my sacrum. Then a sharp wind flings back the grains at my bare legs, so it's like the burn of a cloud of tiny knives.

A runner lopes over, an Irishman but he lives in Durham. See, I was born on a cliff, he tells me. You know,

   I come here and it's like I can feel
   all of my gills opening!

Durham Coast, August 2019
Commissioned by Durham Book Festival
and the National Trust, 2019

About Lew Welch

ARAM SAROYAN

I'm very smart, and over-educated, and so on, but you know – and I can make all kinds of points about that *kinda shit – but what I really would like to do is – wouldn't it be wonderful to write a song or a story that anybody would say at his hearth on any given evening just because he loved the way it went? And that's what I want to do. And I think that that is what poetry is about.*
– Lew Welch, in an interview with David Meltzer, July 17 1969

IN THE SPRING OF 1976, I visited the offices of KPFA, the listener-sponsored radio station in Berkeley, with Donald Allen, Lew Welch's literary executor, editor and publisher, who had been asked by the station to help put together a memorial program devoted to Welch to be aired in May, some five years after his disappearance.

While we were there, Eric Bauersfeld, the station's literary director, played a little of each of the half-a-dozen or so tapes of Welch that were in the station's archives, and there was one in particular that struck me. It was a tape of Gary Snyder, Philip Whalen and Lew Welch discussing how they got by as poets, recorded at the station with a moderator in the spring of 1964 to promote a reading they were about to give together in San Francisco. We just heard a quick few minutes of the tape, but the idea of these three poets who had known each other since their days together at Reed College in the late 1940s all in the same discussion together, seemed almost too good to be true. I remember suggesting to Donald Allen on the spot that the broadcast, which had been titled 'On Bread and Poetry', would make a good book.

A month or so later, while I was visiting Don, a Bolinas neighbour, he asked if I'd like the job of transcribing the tape for him; and during the next several days while engaged in this project, I felt that I began to get to know Welch. While I'd read his collected poems, *Ring of Bone*, and *How I Work as a Poet & Other Essays/Stories/Plays*, as well as the small volume *Trip Trap*, which he shares with Jack Kerouac and Albert Saijo, I had yet to really make up my mind about him. When I read these books during the summer of 1973, having recently finished a novel, I had wondered whether Welch had taken the all-out step of what I thought of just then as a real writer – the step, that is, of accepting one's personality for better or worse. Ironically, there was something about the unremitting craftsmanship of Welch's poems that made me suspect him; I wondered if he'd ever really ended his apprenticeship.

The recording, running a full hour, made me forget about all this almost immediately. 'On Bread and Poetry', with its three interweaving voices – plus the moderator's intelligent and appropriately 'square' questions – was as clear a presentation as I had ever experienced of what I think of as the living tradition in American poetry. The three poets are virtually interviewing each other, and their individual approaches and emphases are supported by a shared sense of poetry as important and integral to a healthy society:

> *Snyder:* I find it very exciting to have some poems, a few poems which I can show to academic types, or say artistic and literary types around San Francisco, and they will say, 'Yes, that's a poem.' And I can also read it or show it to a logger or a seaman, and he will say, 'That's great. Yeah, I like that'.
> *Welch:* Yes, that's one of my standards, too.
> *Whalen:* And that's something that all of us have been able to do, incidentally. I mean a lot of friends of mine have come around and said, 'I showed something of yours to this bum', and so on, and the bum flipped. And it's great.
> *Welch:* The cab drivers like my cab poems. They said, 'Yeah, that's just the way it is. By gosh, you write like that, hunh? That's good'.

As anyone familiar with their work knows, they were not advocating a superficial populism, but rather calling up an awareness of the deeper common ground we share: seaman and intellectual, taxi-driver and poet. And of the three voices, it was Welch's which most surprised and, despite some hesitation and wariness on my part, moved me. He was the least familiar of the three to me. I had long been an admirer of the work of both Philip Whalen and Gary Snyder, but it was Welch's voice that spoke most directly to me as a fellow human amidst the trials and uncertainties of my own life.

Answering a question from the moderator about how the poets related to the 'bulk of the people that you pass on the street, and that you talk to, who don't dress like you, who probably don't think like you, and who probably don't know very much about what you're interested in', Welch said that he had stopped thinking in terms of 'any hip–square division':

> I really used to, and I think it was a great error on my part. I think it was not only inaccurate, but it was immoral. I mean if you start thinking of we-*them*, naturally you cause all kinds of hostilities to rise [...]. And that got badly confused sometime around fifty-eight or nine – there was just too much of

this – of a senseless hostility going back and forth, coming from both sides, about *nothing*.

After I had transcribed the tape, I could no longer identify the craftsmanship of his poems with the tightness of an apprentice afraid to fail. Instead, it came to me how open and full of life his poems and prose were, while at the same time being consistently finely and carefully written. I realized that Welch's craft was not what I had first thought, but rather an implicit part of his generosity as a writer. He wrote so carefully so that everyone could understand him.

A few months later I embarked on a book about Welch because I was interested in how so clear a sense of both poetry and the poet's role, as he articulated it in 'On Bread and Poetry', had evolved. The manuscript was written three decades ago while living with my wife and our three young children in Bolinas. When it was done, I immediately put it aside and undertook writing a 'second draft', *Genesis Angels: The Saga of Lew Welch and the Beat Generation*, which bears little relation to it. The published book, that is, is an overview of the Beat Generation and its central figures (with Lew Welch the main protagonist) written novelistically in a Beat-inflected, Kerouac-style prose.

The first draft, on the other hand, is a study of the life and writing of one writer, Lew Welch, a lesser-known figure among his peers, whose own words dominate the narrative. In our day of exhaustive, minutiae-oriented biographies, this was, of course, a dicey approach. Why would one take it? I had a strong sense that Welch, for all his frailty and his life-long struggle with alcoholism, was as lucid a guide on his own journey *in medias res* as one could wish for. Then too, a point of intersection exists, I think, where the disinterested mind of the genuine artist meets the disinterested mind of the scientist – physicist, neurologist, or psychiatrist. At his best Welch had a capacity for both a laser-like verbal precision and a self-forgetting honesty that one encounters rarely.

More specifically, the way he atomized the creative process seemed to dovetail with the discoveries of the new physics and suggest a common ground. Whether 'creating' had to do with combinations of atoms and molecules or with a poem, at the bottom of both enterprises, it now seemed, was a mirror rather than matter, which led back to self-forgetting, or – perhaps another word for it – consciousness. And Welch, I think, explicates his own engagement as well as Gary Zukav narrates the peregrinations of subatomic particles in *The Dancing Wu-Li Masters*. Here, then, is an excerpt from the first draft that tries to track Welch's precise understanding of the process of poetic genesis:

THE WHOLE THING

During the late sixties, Lew Welch took on the role of Tribal Elder to the hippie culture centered in the Haight-Ashbury neighborhood of San Francisco. Anticipating the over-crowding that eventually led to the disintegration of the community, in the spring of 1967 Welch wrote a piece called 'A Moving Target Is Hard to Hit', which was duplicated by The Communications Company using a Gestetner and distributed free to residents by the Diggers. A current top-forty hit, 'If You're Going to San Francisco (Be Sure to Wear Some Flowers in Your Hair)', seemed to be addressed to young people across the nation, if not the world. Welch wrote:

> When 200,000 folks from places like lima ohio and cleveland and lompoc and visalia and amsterdam and london and moscow and lodz suddenly descend, as they will, on the haight-ashbury, the scene will be burnt down. Some will stay and fight. Some will prefer to leave. My brief remarks are for those who have a way or ways similar to mine: *disperse*. ('A Moving Target is Hard to Hit', 6)

The piece ends:

> [F]or those who have this kind of way, not out of cowardice, but as WAY [...] sitting in the haight-ashbury in all that heat and the terrible crowd you cannot help anyway (maybe), is simple insanity.
> Disperse. Gather into smaller tribes. Use the beautiful land your state and national governments have already set up for you, free. If you want to.
> Most Indians are nomads. The haight-ashbury is not where it's at it's in your head and hands. Take it anywhere.
> ('A Moving Target is Hard to Hit', 7)

That summer, the fabled Summer of Love, Welch wrote an August 9th letter to Gary Snyder, again in Japan, in which he reports on the explosive American scene:

> Well the revolution is finally happening. Detroit and 40 other cities blew up in July – the 1967 total is 70 cities and towns. Marin City, my home town, blew up a weekend ago so bad we thought it prudent to evacuate ourselves [...] It's not so much a racial revolution as a revolution of the poor. Detroit looting was integrated – spade cats helping white cats into the high window. Not so much about colored skin as about colored TV. TV sets scattered all over Detroit by folks who found them too heavy to get home in all that rifle fire.
>
> [I]t's pretty scary living in violence, I really don't want Jeff [his partner Magda Cregg's son] to get hurt, or Magda, but here is where we live and we just get used to rifle fire (every night for more than two months [...]).
> (*I Remain* 144 :2)

About Haight-Ashbury he wrote:

> [T]he Meth Freak hippy pushers have got so big the Mafia is moving in and pushers in the Hashbury are getting murdered. Three at least. *And* the acid is untakeable because it may be STP (an Army drug developed to pacify or wipe out the enemy, the trip goes on for 72 hours and 4 of my friends, some of them very strong, are now in loony bins), not to mention the bad shit LSD with Meth in it. Gary, people, good ones, are blowing their minds irreversibly. Like, gone. Away.
> Of course there are also the beautiful things. Like George Harrison and his wife appeared in the Hashbury and it was two hours before they were recognized. Then George led a huge meaningless parade singing and banging his guitar. He is stone serious about his teacher Ravi Shankar, who, naturally, does not condone drugs. George had purple glasses, in the shape of a heart. His wife is very wild looking. [...] pretty, granny glasses, et al.

In this tumultuous period, Welch seemed to discern a kind of urban apocalypse, a chaotic, disintegrating 'last stand' of America's urban-industrial era. He wrote a piece called 'Final City/Tap City' for the June 28-July 11, 1968 issue of the *San Francisco Oracle* in which he foresaw an end to the cities:

> We face great holocausts, terrible catastrophies [sic], all American cities burned from within, and without.
> However, our beautiful Planet will germinate – underneath this thin skin of City, Green will come on to crack our sidewalks! Stinking air will blow away at last! The bays flow clean! ('Final City/Tap City', 20)

In the face of the impending disaster he envisions, Welch's love for nature, his enduring faith in the planet itself, informs and modulates virtually all of his later writing with an increasing emphasis. This dimension of his work and thought during the sixties sets it apart from the revolutionary pronouncements so endemic to the period. When Paul Krassner asked to reprint 'Final City/Tap City' in *The Realist*, Welch revised it and added a section in which he focuses and elaborates on a cultural chasm that goes beyond 'the generation gap' given play in the national media:

> I always admired Arthur Koestler, and always was enraged by him. I knew him to be smart, well read, and almost pathologically honest. Also, he cared a lot about the things I wanted to know. None of this changed the fact that I knew Koestler was wrong. 'Wrong' is a very good word. Very few educated people still know how to use it.
> Just two weeks ago I found Koestler giving himself away to my sense of his wrongness. He says, in *Yogi & the Commissar*, that we are a 'vulnerable animal, living on a hostile planet'. Clearly this man has never looked at his own two hands. Has never known the miracle of his human eyes. Does not know he is the only animal which can out-climb a mountain goat (as the northwest Indians do, chinning themselves on quarter-inch ledges in the rock, till they drive the goat to where the goat must fall). Can do that, and also swim. Can run with the halter in his hand until the horse drops dead. Can curl up into a ball, as the fox does, let the snow cover him, for warmth, and make it through a blizzard on Mt. Shasta. As John Muir did.
> Koestler doesn't know the skin he stands in, the meat he is, and he doesn't know the ground he's standing on. What, possibly, can he tell us about anything else? [...]
> Koestler knows he's wrong, he's always cringing about it. He is the scapegoat, here, not because he's the worst, but because he's among the best of those who make articulate the European Mind we must (at pain of death) reject.
> Camus and Sartre make the same errors, but have no humbleness.
> ('Final City/Tap City', 17–18)

The sense that direct experience of the world is the necessary basis of sound thinking or writing goes back to Welch's piece 'Poems and Remarks' (*I Remain* 40–1:27), which he prepared for William Carlos Williams's visit to

Reed College in 1950. There the young poet espoused the Chinese ladder, as opposed to Plato's ladder, as a model for his own development. Rather than seeking the idealized, perfected Platonic forms, the Chinese model proposed the mature stage of *Sh'n-Yee* in which an artist achieved an integration of technique and subject matter taken directly from life.

Speaking in broad terms, this distinction sometimes seems to lie at the heart of the difference between what might be characterized as the East and West coast styles in American art. On the East Coast, where what Welch calls the 'European Mind' is traditionally more dominant, the Platonic ideal of perfected form seems to hold sway. In poetry, the work of Wallace Stevens or James Merrill might be regarded as prototypes.

On the West Coast, where the Asian influence is stronger, the Chinese emphasis on experience as the source and subject of art has created another standard. The poetry of Kenneth Rexroth and Gary Snyder might be regarded as embodiments of this Western archetype. Welch's emphasis on making his work accessible to the general public, recalling the example of the Tang Dynasty poet Po Chu-I, is among his most important contributions to the tradition. In addition to speaking to the counter-culture, he addressed the public at large in two reviews for the *San Francisco Chronicle* in which he discussed the work of two of his peers, Richard Brautigan and Philip Whalen.

In his review of Whalen's collected poetry, *On Bear's Head*, printed in June 1969, he wrote of his experience when he circulated a Whalen poem 'Further Notice' among his fellow workers at Montgomery Ward. The poem goes:

> I can't live in this world
> And I refuse to kill myself
> Or let you kill me
>
> The dill plant lives, the airplane
> My alarm clock, this ink
> I won't go away
>
> I shall be myself –
> Free, a genius, an embarrassment
> Like the Indian, the buffalo
>
> Like Yellowstone National Park.   (*On Bear's Head* 46–45)

Welch recalled:

> Soon, 'Yellowstone National Park' was used by secretaries, bosses, whatever kind of wage slave as a way of showing their integrity when things got tough. These poems are useful. ('Philip Whalen as Yellowstone National Park', 26)

In the July 1969 interview with him conducted by David Meltzer, Welch quoted the dedicatory poem 'to the memory of Gertrude Stein & William Carlos Williams' that introduces *Ring of Bone*:

> I WANT THE WHOLE THING, the moment
> when what we thought was rock, or
> sea
> became clear Mind, and
>
> what we thought was clearest Mind really
> *was* that glancing girl, that
> swirl of birds …
>
> (all of that)
>
> AND AT THE SAME TIME that very poem
> pasted in the florist's window
>
> (as Whalen's *I wanted to bring you this Jap Iris* was)
>
> carefully retyped and
> put right out there on Divisadero St.
>
> just because the florist thought it pretty,
>
> that it might remind of love, that it might sell flowers …
>
> The line, 'Tangled in Samsara!'
> (*Ring of Bone* v)

This poem, dated 'Mt. Tamalpais 1970', clearly encapsulates Welch's poetics. The first part presents his vision of the state of consciousness he identifies as the source of poetry: 'the moment' in which the mind is 'JOINING with whatever-is–*out-there*', as he wrote to Donald Allen in 1960 (*I Remain* 207 :1). This is the moment spoken of in Buddhist literature in which there is no separation between the observer and what-is-observed, the essentially wordless and eternal 'moment' that occurs in forgetting oneself (*Ring of Bone* v).

The second part of the poem, beginning 'AND AT THE SAME TIME', presents Welch's vision of the proactive function of poetry in society at large. The poem by Whalen 'pasted in the florist window […] that it might remind of love,/that it might sell flowers' has a 'useful' place in the social scheme of things. Born out of an essentially timeless experience of communion between the poet and the world, the poem has a civic function in the time and place of its making, tangling itself in Samsara, the worldly sphere. Near the end of the interview with Meltzer, Welch says: The poem is not the vision. The vision is the source of the poem. The poem is the chops, but the real chops are being able to go across that river and come back with something that is readable:

> Lew's a healthy thing. He is a healthy thing. And it doesn't even matter if you burn yourself out, and drink too much, and commit suicide. People do that anyway. Cat-skinners do that. Advertising executives do that. That's part of some of the hazards you run in life. And the hazards you run in, so to speak, the psychological impurities that are in the material that have to burn out sooner or later.
>
> (Gary Snyder, in an interview with the author, March 1977)

In Praise Of Birds

VAHNI CAPILDEO

In praise of high-contrast birds, purple bougainvillea thicketing the golden oriole.

In praise of civic birds, vultures cleansing the valleys, hummingbird logos on the tails of propeller planes; in praise of adaptable birds, the herring gull that demonstrates its knowledge of how to use a box junction, and seems to want to cross the road.

In praise of birds eaten by aeroplane engines; in praise of birds trained to hunt drones; in praise of birds that, having nothing to do with human processes, crash aeroplanes.

In praise of suicidal birds, brown ground doves forgetful of wingèdness, in front of cars, slowly crossing the road.

In praise of perse birds like fish smashing out of a bowl.

In praise of talk being cheep, and in praise of men who shut up about birds.

In praise of birds of death and communication, Garuda the almost-but-more-than-an-eagle vehicle of the darkly bejewelled and awfully laughing Lord of Death.

In praise of badly drawn birds.

In praise of white egrets, sitting on mud, hippos, and lines about old age.

In praise of Old English birds of exile, the gannet's laughter, swathes of remembered seabirds booming and chuckling, the urgent cuckoo blazing on about summer, mournful and mindblowing, driving the sailor over the edge towards impossible targets, scornful of gardens, salty about city life – I can't stand not setting off; far is seldom far enough.

In praise of a turn of good cluck.

In praise of the high-dancing birds carried on the heads of masqueraders and built by wirebenders to carry the spirit of an archipelago of more than seven thousand isles.

In praise of grackles quarrelling on the lawn.

In praise of unbeautiful birds abounding in Old Norse, language of scavenging ravens, thought and memory, a treacherous duo. The giantess down from the mountain complained – I couldn't sleep in a coastal bed because of the yammering of waterfowl. Every morning that blasted seagull wakes me.

In praise of the peacocks invading the car park at the Viking conference in York, warming their spread tails on the bodies of cars.

In praise of the early bird who liberates the dewy worm from glaucous grass.

In praise of birds of timetelling: green-rumped parrots for morning, kiskadees dipping at night: and the absence of birds of timetelling, the unreeled horror of humanly meaningless time.

In praise of the bird of the soul that flies out when the body is molested, and in praise of that bird recalling the abuse room as if perched on the highest point of the pinewood press.

In praise of the blueblack grassquit, which is inky and small.

In praise of the albatross, in praise of the double doors to a swimming baths hall.

In praise of birds of concussion, notes in the air being all the brain can cope with.

In praise of birds as edible and in praise of birds as angels and in praise of birds as stones and in praise of Thoth the Ibis.

In praise of the birds of climate change, forest warblers bringing a new song to the suburbs, late-leaving Arctic tern teenagers blizzarding the beach.

In praise of ducking and diving, and without praise of the cruelty of quills.

In praise of birds that are not punctuation, that are not calendars, that are not words.

In praise of birds that occupy and disrupt a lyrical musical staff.

In praise of birds that singing still do shit, shitting ever singing, above a low-rent skylight, on a diet of chips.

In praise of triangulation and three unseen corncrakes by whose calls guests may recognize the way to the house on the tipsy hill.

In praise of increasingly grotesque fossil remains of proto-birds, and the discovery of normality as never having been such.

In praise of birds plucked for dream armour, flame fur, plate plume, and in praise of women who fight like cranes and swans.

In praise of thump and slime.

In praise of fine feathers, prophecies, and export regulations.

In praise of Quetzalcoatl. Tremble to say more.

In praise of the birds of prognostication, gutted, magnetic, or altering their calls.

In praise of rare and less showy doctors refraining from labelling immigrants as insane or aggressive, as more regularly spotted doctors may be observed to do.

In praise of Suibhne, driven mad by the dinning of church bells, yearning for his dinner of unchlorinated cress.

In praise of Suibhne's flights crossing land and water, and Suibhne's poetry crossing time and language, to and from, tidalectic, praise.

Once more on Value and English Lit.

WALTER BRUNO

IN A RECENT CONVERSATION in the *Chronicle of Higher Education*, Michael Clune took on Gabrielle Starr and Kevin Dettmar, in a debate over skills development in English, and whether fictional literature was relevant for employers.

It was prompted by the current soul-searching in English, amidst an academy turning more and more to *training* and away from literature. In all of this, the debaters agreed that curriculum must have a value, or a *use-value* for employment. Still, employers were sceptical of the outcomes. This was not a minor issue, since English enrollments are cratering, and professorial ranks, thinning.

For their part, Professors Starr and Dettmar argued that English had *employment value* even as graduates went into non-academic jobs. For them, value in literary study was generated by critical thinking, and critical thinking came from readers making their own meanings of texts. Furthermore, they insisted that classical canons could not do that; critical thinking came from reading voices that were new to literature or revealed by the new deconstructions. They saw this as a battle between the tastes of older elites, *drilled* into students, and *empathetic* awareness, brought on by new stories about new people:

Sit in on any English class and you'll hear a lot about value – about the value of literature in pushing the boundaries of empathy; about the efficacy of poetry in encouraging thorough, expansive engagement, rather than minimal, uniform assessment; about the moral weight of fiction in a world that may be post-truth. Value is certainly front and centre, but not the value that only belongs to a few initiates in a small, narrow sphere.

Dr Clune was unconvinced, and asked what Silicon Valley, taken as a sample employer, expects from the curriculum, aside from the alleged social empathy from Starr and Dettman. At the end of the day, he suggests, the Valley wants efficient communicators, not workers who can parse text for how it constructs meaning from stories of under-represented populations – read by the same populations (my paraphrase).

What bothered me, though, was that both sides took *use-value* of English literature as a given, although they disagreed on what it was. I concur that use-value exists; however, I suggest its presence is relatively weak in the genesis of literature. In any case, use-value folds into the wider outcome I call *literacy* (an unavoidable tautology). Furthermore, it can be achieved by programmes run out of a communications department. And not only through text: films, to name but one other medium, can reveal *layered meanings* in every scene.

At any rate, for the opponents of Dr Clune, the value of English Lit was that it engaged readers with diversified narratives to which they might have been indifferent, because of their education, or because of their upbringing in hegemonic classes of people. Further, it was the student's private task to make meaning; we were alleged to be in a post-truth world, where less empowered views have been historically suppressed. In the end, this new matrix of experience and meanings constituted *empathy*. Furthermore, the teaching of poetry (until 1980) had been limited to technocratic specialists, obsessed with craft, which cramped wider meaning. A poem had form and meter, and perhaps pattern and a metaphor or two. The social genesis of the work was both flagrant and ignored.

Already, I see a difficulty. What if I had read *Paradise Lost* and empathized with the character of Satan? Did my empathy come from a family tradition of atheism? Or, from the fact that Satan is referenced in the text as *he*, and I am also a *he*? Did empathy come from the poet's nonconformism, or was it his envy of male heroism, revolt, and pride?

Let's take a second example. What if I liked a novel with diversity, say, one about a rich Ethiopian who is fragile, and who is bullied by a poor schoolmate. Did I previously think there were no rich bullied Ethiopian children? Did I imagine all Ethiopian bullies as categorically poor? If not, then why was the novel transformative? What were its *values*?

Pondering this, I wonder why we talk about values in the first place. Value is about judgement and transaction. However, artistic standards evolved separately from social transaction, and steadily toward a sense of wonder and release. They were independent of use-value, and gleaned from a search for Truth. Nowhere was it proposed that a rich woman, for example, could not share the truth of a man or a slave-girl.

One could sum it up with a rule: well-crafted work reveals a Truth deeper than the values that contend in society. Hegel called it artistic *geist*. A century earlier, Alexander Pope had said this:

First follow NATURE, and your judgment frame
By her just standard, which is still the same. . .
Life, force, and beauty, must to all impart,
At once the source, and end, and test of art.

In this, truth emerges from nature, but from essential nature, not nature composed. This idea has bounced around philosophy for millennia, and honed our sense of the *enduring* and the *beautiful*. Yet Starr and Dettmar don't argue from that, and Clune doesn't take it up, perhaps, for brevity. He limits himself to mentioning the weaknesses of his critics' view of empathy.

In addition to an insufficient basis for empathy, Starr and Dettmar are vehemently *anti-Truth*. Artistic truth has no inherent moral or ethical centre, and ethics are still the concern. They speak ambiguously about a 'post-truth world', which they neither condemn nor deny, but set empathy as a replacement for Truth. In the end, fictional Truth is eclipsed by moral instruction, which, as seen above, they call fiction's 'moral weight'.

Finally, Starr-Dettmar's view of *craft* follows a bias of historical criticism, which tends to demote the craftsman. Craft, suggest Starr-Dettmar, was a refuge for the dispassionate and neutral snob, which a teacher can never be. But this can be a false dichotomy: craft is never cold or foreign to empathy – it interacts with it.

Nor is high craft ostentation; it triggers the conscience. As thinkers have posited since Aristotle, the craft of writing is a testable network of intertwined empathies.

I've observed that our poetic heritage was written by elite poets. Yet the same poets often spoke of nature and the poor and the decay of elites. In ancient Rome, the dissolute Catullus was warning his friend Aurelius not to abuse servant boys and vouching for the morals of labourers, more reliable than their masters'. As for nature, he found his boat's voice in the shore trees that had furnished its timbers.

This poses similar questions: did the Roman elites have to read poems about forests and plebeians in order to peg them as subjects? Or to want to know about them? Probably not. The poet obeys his muse sooner than he obeys a tutor or a research grant.

Observing this, classical philosophers admitted subjects from an innate curiosity, all the while troubling the waters with what they called poetic beauty. From that, they might compare *inhering* Truth with value-laden manners, and do it equally for class, sex, gender, and other identities.

Let's first turn to gender – if, for no other reason, than that it concerns the majority of students. All right, what about literary *gender*? Has it always been sex-bound? And what about history; how does *contemporaneity* affect writing and critiquing gender? Do we need English departments to stress that, and to tilt readings towards or against certain texts?

Let's do an experiment. Set aside, for a moment, one of today's gender billboards – say, Eve Ensler – and read from the male-authored canon of yesterday. I suggest we go to Honoré de Balzac's novel *Eugénie de Grandet*.

In that book from 1833, you have a world of peasants, nobles, bourgeois, males and females, fools and cads, and a repressed daughter who wins the day over her father, who is the local miser. In the end, she triumphs as he fails. That's in an 1833 male canon; however, the book is a reprise of Shakespeare and Molière, and *commedia* and a line of classics – nothing really new. What about gay women? Set aside today's self-conscious texts, and go read *La Femme de Paul* (Paul's Wife), a story from Guy de Maupassant published in 1881. In that, a Paris watering-hole is conquered by a boatload of lesbian revellers, who are initially greeted with mixed emotions, but finally welcomed for their fast and forward lives.

On the other hand, they have a friend named Paul; he is driven to tragedy. Let's consider that. The Maupassant heroes are lesbians; but Paul, their (unintended) victim, is a young man, frail and conventional. With whom did the reader empathize in 1881? And to whom do we relate today? The answer – for both eras – should be the same: we relate to both. And indeed, given a classical education, the answer for the majority of readers is *both*.

The point, of course, is not to fuss about value, but to suggest that the canon, that body of exemplary work, from eras we are supposed to de-emphasise, represents a sui-generis gain for students. It instructs them on the sly but suspect pretence of *all values*; and it teaches us to value the beautiful.

Say *Elbow*, Say *Heart* and other poems

SUZANNAH V. EVANS

Say *Elbow*, Say *Heart*

Spritsail, butt block, camber, centreboard,
aligned ribs, apron, gaff rigged sloop, breasthook.

The boatbuilders balance by curved pieces of timber
(oak for the keel, pitch pine
for hull planking, larch for masts and spars).
They let language fall from their tongues,
let it shape the movement of their hands.

Chine construction, scantlings, sap wood, rowlock,
topside, capstan, bowsprit, fender, jib, footwell.

I say *elbow*, and they think of the curved piece
of frame at the turn of the bilge, I say *heart*,
and they picture the centre of a section of timber.

Pintle, peak up, planking, rabbet, rigging,
oakum, middle futtock, limber hole, lodging knee.

The language is worked into the wood as they move,
mahogany murmuring with the sound of *canvas*,
carlins, *clinker*, *coaming*, *cradle*, *crook*,
taking on the shine of *seam*, *scuppering*, in place of varnish,
settling down into the hull of the yacht soothed
by the words *starboard*, *spiling batten*, *shutter plank*.

Chocks away, *heave-up*, *nearly there* they call out
in their sleep, empty hands grasping rope,
lidded eyes imaging the sight of a red hull inching
onto a slipway – and as the dream fades away,
and the sun eases up over the harbour,
the words *brightwork brightwork brightwork*
lap at the corners of their rooms.

Slipway

Your other names are less lovely to me – boat ramp,
launch, boat deployer. As the rain slips in, sluicing over
silt and sawdust in the harbour, I think of slippages, how
your name could slip to skidway, or siltway, or saltway,
or softway, or tiltway. I've seen you slide into the water,
lowering yourself with an easy song, a sweet whining, a
slow clanking; I've seen your wooden posts sink deeper like
fins. There are other lovely things about you: your timber
cradle, how you hold the hulls of boats so closely, how
you keep your chocking stable, and whistle at the sight
of a wooden deck. They call you a Heave-Up Slip, but the
only heaving is done by the men around you, who lower
poles, wind winches, puff and glance up at the sky. You are
serene, slipping into the water with the ease of a seal from
a rock, moving your great whale body through the harbour,
stretching like a spine, singing your sweet, sweet song.

Barnacle Oblong

Having been told by the boatbuilders
that there is no name for the hollowed space
between the keel and the rudder,
for that oblong space that is like the body of a fish,
the space that peeks out behind the white and aqua
hull of the boat that Jasper saved, the little hillyard,
the little 9-metre hillyard named Puffin,
having been told that the space is for a propeller,
but that there is no name for the space,
I cast around and ask the boatyard strollers,
the visiting tourists, the women with pushchairs,
the men with long cameras, the children with caps,
what they might call that space, standing next to
Win's Clair de Lune, that beautiful white boat
with the peeling hull, the rusting rudder,
and that unnamed space peering out behind,
and they say, laughing at first, looking round,
rudder-hole, *prop gap*, *propeller housing*,
and Andy, passing, says *wiggle-space*, *spin space*,
and Julie says *prop shaft exit*, sounding technical,
and then serious men who pass say *propeller aperture*,
rudder gap, and one wonderful woman says
The Void, and walks off, silently, and I think *moon void*,
and a laughing man says *The No Idea*,
the nautical gap, and another man says it looks
just like a bow, an archer's bow, and then words build
and pour: *boat crescent*, *hull crescent*,
The C, *The Cake Slice*, *rusted teardrop*,
interrupted moon (I think, as someone says *moon*,
then *moon cut*), *The Reverse D*, *The Knotty Question*,
spare space, *spin spot*, *Phillip*, *Knobber*,
and one woman who used to be an English teacher
says *aerated vista*, and one man, scratching his head,
says *The Hole & Gap*, like the space is a pub,
a beloved space, and a passing French woman says
l'aileron, the word lilting out into the air,
and the German girl pauses, thinks, says *das Hörnchen*,
and the man she's with says *back wing*, and now
the boatyard is alive with words taking wing:
media luna, *navigation alcove*, *pickle moon*,
sickle moon, *propeller crevice*, *cor blimey*,
The D-Space, *thrust capsule*, *half moon*,
and I think *griddle*, *barnacle oblong*.

Three Poems

CHRISTINE ROSEETA WALKER

If Me Did Know

I didn't know what possessed me
to take the seat of a stranger.

I was on a plane from Montego Bay
when a woman asked

me to exchange seats. I am a good
Jamaican, so I did.

when the plane stopped in London
a man in white shirt

with a pen in him pocket escort me
through a back gate.

'you didn't eat your meal', him say.
'So you must be a drug

mule!' A drug-mule? Is what him say
to me? I am a forty nine

year old woman, from the gully. The
only mule I know was

Maas Allen's old donkey, who had one
good foot and a chewed

off ear. Him showed me to a doctor's
bed and told me to let down

me hair. To take off me clothes,
to show me-self like pickney

chasing fresh air. When me holler 'after
me no done noting!'

him left him chair and came back with a
woman. 'Is your name

Wendy Martin?' I told them it wasn't.
She opened my passbook,

saw Tanya Weir. 'You're saying you're
not Martin?' 'Is that me say

is hear you can't hear?' We went on
like this till the tea them

bring was a cup of ice. And me start
to forget why me board

the blue and white bird, in the first
place. The woman gave

me back me clothes and told me to
enjoy my stay. I could

a cut me eyes on her, but I couldn't
wait. I saw me brother standing

far away, him mobile phone to him ear.
Him waved, came running over.

I couldn't look him in the face or tell
him why me was so so late.

The Swivel Chair

The old lady had once had a daughter that died
in New York. Her body was shipped home and buried
under a jackfruit tree. Her apartment stripped
and a swivel chair sent across the Caribbean sea.
The chair arrived on a Friday in a large brown box.
The old lady loved the chair because it showed
the life her daughter had. She placed the chair
on the verandah next to her wicker bench.
All summer the chair on its metal column
turned and turned and turned. The old lady feared
that the chair would cease to be
a swivel chair if the turning did not stop.
In the heat of the sun, the chair turned and turned
and turned. Its molasses coloured oil seeped up
from its base as the chair turned and turned.
The neighbours who came to the old lady's house
watched the chair turn right round, then left, and right
round again. The old lady was kind and the local children
enjoyed sitting on her verandah eating mangoes
and singing ring-game songs.
The children also liked spinning on the foreign chair:
never had they seen a chair that goes round and round
like a merry-go-round. The old lady knew that the chair
would not last if the turning did not stop and would
ask the children not to spin as much. But the children would
not listen. Each day they'd come to the old lady's verandah
and whirl and whirl on the swivel chair, laughing, whooping,
and singing. They did not know what the chair meant.
The old lady did not tell them that the chair had belonged to
her only daughter. Instead, she would ask them
not to spin as much, but the swivel chair turned
and turned until one day
the old lady's soft voice faltered. She did not ask the children
to stop as she had done before. She watched them turn
and turn the memory of her child into creaks and oil.
And each day the children came and sat down
in pairs singing: dirty bus, dirty bus, round and round,
donkey want water, wash him down.
As the sun was setting behind the sea,
the chair began to squeak and squeak, as if
the voice of her dead daughter was calling from within
the leather seat. The children heard the squeak
but kept on spinning and spinning and spinning.
The old lady watched in silence as the metal column
grew longer and longer. It rose up until she could see its
metal tip sharp. The seat tumbled to the floor.
The children were still clinging on when it crashed
to the ground. They squealed and laughed,
and giggled. The children tried to push the column back
inside the base, but could not. They drifted off,
leaving the chair in halves. The old lady watched the children go
one by one. She looked at the broken chair and thought
of her daughter's voice and the children's song
and felt something swell inside her heart. She called her son
to take the base and the seat to the back room and lock them in
with the bed-foot and frame of her daughter's things.
Whenever the old lady passed by the door she could hear
the children's song haunting the room. At night when she could
not sleep, she would hear her daughter's voice singing
in a foreign accent: *dirty bus, dirty bus, round and round,*
donkey wants water, wash him down.

Mischief

I'm not going to tell you who poisoned the old
Tamarind tree. I'm not ready to disclose who was swinging from the
branch or what happened before they landed.
I'm not going to tell you about the empty fishing boat,
sinking. I'm not ready to tell you what happened to the shark that pulled
it in. I'm not going to tell you who tied the plastic around the shark's head,
or who started the fire under granny's bed.
I'm not ready to tell you who smoked the last cigarette, the tobacco,
and the seaweed from the cabinet. I'm not going to tell you who stole the money
from the letter, the mattress, and the saving can.
I'm not going to tell you who drank the Appleton rum,
then hid the bottle under the drum.
I'm not ready to disclose who muddied the white blankets on the wire,
drying. I'm not going to tell you who wore your favorite slipper,
or whose dog chewed up the leather strap.
I'm not going to tell you who set fire to the cat's tail
or who puts it out with a blanket from the trunk.
I'm not ready to disclose who ate both
jonnie-cakes and the four chicken legs,
for uncle Sam's dinner.
I'm not going to tell you how I know all this.
don't ask me to squeal who done it!
No, I can't tell you about the match-sticks, the toxin
or the rope on the old fruit tree.
I can't tell you whose boat it was
or where the shark ended up.
I can't tell you about the rum, the weed
or who mixed in the mud.
I'm not going to tell you where I saw your English money,
spending. It wasn't your dog that bites through your slipper,
and I'm not going to tell you whose it was
because if I did, then it wouldn't be mischief.

Anthracite

Martin Elliott

1.
For now, I only dream of Anthracite
gemlike but hot & low of smoke,
brought to the house on Barcock's lorry
– a whole half ton checked in by tallyman me.
9 years old, I'm looking to kick some slack.
No such luck. Only slurry.
Coloured by their trade were Barcock's heavers
with boot-black faces – & helmed and caped
like Foreign Legionnaires –
but hardly debonair, hoisting hessian
sackloads heavier than I. We likewise
had our annual chimney sweep
another dark-grained serf of soot
whose thoroughgoing

sockety-handled
bristle brush
was also scanned for
(yes, again, by vigilante me)
above our chimney stack:
Look it's like a head!
like someone's head
surprised & looking down
on all the rush!

2.
Since train or barge had brought the coal
from Rhondda Valley, Yorkshire, Nottingham
we met no actual coalface colliers,
nor boys – called Dai in Wales – who pulled the dans.

The loads shot-off at local depots
made pyramids beside the tracks
– which is to say the mining folk
were rare to us as Pharaohs might have been.
Except on newsreels, strikers overground,
we had no view of pitface lives
until we watched Morel of Sons & Lovers,
his privilege of nightly scrubs in zinc,
his weekly midnight drunks, his marriage soured,
as played against the grain by Trevor Howard.
Medicine had small regard
for men in mines.
Low in the tabloid scares
came lung fibrosis
– occupational hazard of the pits.
Hitting the headlines
was infantile paralysis,
caught in swimming pools
by children –
poliomyelitis saw off
silicosis.
In later years the pitmen had hot showers,
male-voice choirs, importantly a weekly wage,
ploughing no more in the stones of hill farms,
less sick with inbreeding as Thomas (R.S.)
inscribed the Welsh. Instead we heard Cwm
Rhondda: watched Dewi Bebb, Gareth Edwards,
J.J. Williams, J.P.R. playing off the scrum.

3.
Oliver, my age, priced at three pound ten,
was 'articled', almost, to a villain sweep
before good fortune came, a silken handkerchief –
the pocketable Artful Dodger.
'Olivers' up chimbleys bare as dancers,
grew knees & elbows soled as if with hide,
choked on dampened fires lit to smoke them out
if in the flue they lapsed or fell asleep.
Their child's disease was scrotal cancer.

4.
Coal-merchants, where you paid your bill,
were lock-up wooden sheds by Tube-line stops –
my uppity widowed mother worked one time
as clerk for Barcock. She'd take a formal pad
and thereupon she'd write your quarterly receipt
in High School sixth form educated hand
with carbon copy. 'This is for your peat.'
Ironically warmed by paraffin,
she used the LT Tube's facilities
& walked the Barcock daily takings,
coins & notes and cheques,
to Barclays' High Street branch –
whilst I, home early, filled a hod with coke
to feed the kitchen stove, for cooking & our baths.

5.
Our house had *heorths*. That in our dining room
had white portico pillars, a mantel
of mahogany, blue tile surrounds.
By reason of impoverished gentility
it witnessed breakfast, lunch, homework, dinner,
the household ironing. Come winter nights
tending the flames, we utilized
the bronze paraphernalia:
fireguard, fender, poker, tongs.
The Clean Air Act ignored,
Aberfan's disaster yet to come,
we did not make laudations
to newer deities.
Our *crookèd Smoakes*, such as they were,
from our *blest Altars*
though not of cedar
as in Cymbeline
sought old gods' nostrils
where London met green pastures in the night
above our own coal face of Anthracite.

Of Lizzie, Cal & Dolphin

TONY ROBERTS

'Surely good writers write all possible wrong'
– 'Summer Between Terms'

'IT IS FAR MORE DIFFICULT to live one's life than to write about it', remarked Nadezhda Mandelstam in a letter to Robert Lowell. This observation was perhaps least appropriate to Lowell, for whom the life and the work were largely synonymous. Over his last seven years – the English years – that life and the poetry clashed head on.

Greatly influential through his career, and often depicted, were his three marriages: to writers Jean Stafford (from 1940 to 1948), to Elizabeth Hardwick, 'Lizzie' (1949 to 1972) and to Lowell's 'dolphin', Lady Caroline Blackwood (1972 to 1977). All three marriages had floundered, undermined by the bipolar disorder that dogged Lowell's life. The first ended in drink and infidelity after Lowell's bout of Catholic zealotry.

The second marriage has been regarded by biographers – ever since Ian Hamilton's brilliant but tart *Robert Lowell: A Biography* in 1982 – as offering a stabilising relationship with the supportive, exploited Hardwick. There are dissenting opinions. Her 'New York Times' obituary in 2007 referred to the marriage as 'restless and emotionally harrowing,' while Lowell's friend and collaborator Frank Bidart (whom Hardwick could be hostile toward) has been at pains to suggest that 'Lizzie was supportive but she could be incredibly difficult too'. Bidart said of his time with them during the editing of Lowell's *Notebook*: 'They absolutely did not know how to talk to each other.' Lowell's third marriage, to Blackwood, intense and chaotic, effectively ended shortly before his death in 1977 when he had returned to New York and Hardwick.

Lowell was, after all, a thoroughly American poet. It is evident in his thematic and prosodic preoccupations and his 'all-outness' in living the role. The trajectory of his career had been from the explosive *Lord Weary's Castle* (1946), with its 'American version of heroic poetry' (Frederick Seidel), to the game-changing *Life Studies* (1959), winner of the National Book Award. This confirmed Lowell's status as the premier post-war American poet, a position consolidated by *For the Union Dead* (1964), a collection offering both public protest and private angst.

Problems had accelerated for Lowell when the 'tranquilized Fifties' turned into the divisive Sixties and the poet – by now a leading literary liberal conscience – became exhausted by the demands made upon him by renown and health. In a poem to their daughter, 'Harriet', he recorded ironically the premature ageing that had become his posture:

> we rest from all discussion, drinking, smoking,
> pills for high blood, three pairs of glasses –soaking
> in the sweat of our hard-earned supremacy,
> offering a child our leathery love. We're fifty,
> and free!

Committed to protest, Lowell participated in the March on the Pentagon, his efforts lauded in Norman Mailer's *The Armies of the Night* (1968). (Amused by the depiction, Lowell reported, 'Later, I wrote him I hoped we'd remain as good friends in life as we were in fiction'.) In 1968 he turned to politics, campaigning for his friend Eugene McCarthy who was engaged in a bid for the Democratic nomination, and then becoming briefly intimate with Kennedy family members.

Some argue – in error I believe – the first signs of Lowell's descent came in 1967 with *Near the Ocean*, which contained his last classic, overtly public poem, 'Waking Early Sunday Morning'. Then came the sonnet sequences of *Notebook 1967–68* and its various manifestations from 1969–73 – with Lowell no poem was ever truly finished. The unrhymed, blank verse sonnets he adopted divided the critics, while he himself felt they allowed more latitude. The form 'can stride on stilts, or talk', he reckoned. Equally importantly it could capture something of the flux of life and memory, though the division between public and private experience is porous. So the poem 'Anne Dick 2. 1936' begins with the Anschluss, touches on Lowell's intention to marry and then – via the view from her family's bay window to M.I.T. – the painter Claude, Nero and Christ (I am reminded of his suggestion in a 1949 letter to George Santayana that for the 'cryptic' poems of his peers, 'It might be profitable to go into illogical associative structures'.)

On leave from teaching at Harvard in 1970, the Lowell's visited Italy. While Hardwick and Harriet returned to New York, Lowell flew to England to take up a fellowship at All Souls College, Oxford. He explained in conversation with Ian Hamilton in 1971 that this was no 'protest against conditions in America, though here there's more leisure, less intensity, fierceness. Everyone feels that; after ten years living on front lines, in New York, I'm rather glad to dull the glare'. The glare he referred to – the violence in the city itself – extended to strained race relations, the aggressive opposition to the Vietnam War that had polarized society, and his own dabbling in politics. Coming to England was tantamount to taking a vacation from his Furies, he said.

A week after arriving he met Caroline Blackwood. This would be no vacation, no passing infidelity. In her late short story, 'An Influx of Poets' – a thinly veiled recounting of her tempestuous marriage to Lowell – Jean Stafford offered the shrewd insight that 'infatuation acquires its history and literature in minutes'. This seems to have been the case with Lowell and Blackwood. As aristocratic as Lowell could wish and a member of the Guinness family, Blackwood was also currently on her second marriage. The thirty-eight-year-old writer, a self-destructive socialite, remembered that after the Faber party in his honour Lowell moved into her Chelsea house in Redcliffe Square 'instantly, that night'. He took up a teaching position at Essex University and two years later – after the birth of their child – they married.

The following year, 1973, *The Dolphin* appeared, bringing with it the controversy that has lingered. The recently published *The Dolphin: Two Versions, 1972-1973* and *The Dolphin Letters*, 1970–1979 – both edited by the indefatigable Saskia Hamilton – allow the reader to explore these last seven years of Lowell's life. While the poems offer his perspective, the letters, like the biographies, redress the balance somewhat, giving Hardwick her own impressive voice. On the other hand Caroline Blackwood, whom the Lowells had known briefly in New York as a silent dinner guest, enters almost exclusively as subject (One might go to *Dangerous Muse* by Nancy Schoenberger (2001) for a lively account of Blackwood's eventful life and 'ragged beauty').

Critical attention is still focused on the use of Hardwick's letters and phone calls in *The Dolphin*, lines from which appear in some form or other in as many as fifteen of the poems. Most seem voiced by Lowell to shape the narrative. There is cold logic in a poet who is looking for verisimilitude (or 'half-fiction') eyeing up his wife's letters when writing about their break-up. It is a temptation many would stifle, just as they would feel inauthentic if voicing the injured party. This is the greater reason for Hardwick's anger. She would much later distance herself, calling the poems from her letters 'quite silly' and adding amusingly, 'they seem to have been under the reign of Lowell's famous habit of revision'. At the time this was not the case. Where in 'Marriage', for example, she is quoted as saying *'not that I wish you entirely well, far from it'* we find the hurt excusable – and yet we learn from Hamilton that her line actually was, 'I don't entirely wish you well, far from it, of course'. While the casual reader may not notice, the poet has moved the 'entirely' to add force to it.

Why did Lowell pursue publication when he knew the damage it could do to those he loved? The answer lies in a letter to Christopher Ricks from March 1972: the book 'needn't be published, but I feel fully clogged by the possibility of not'. Later he would tell Bishop rather dramatically, 'I couldn't bear to have my book (my life) wait inside me like a dead child'. Mary McCarthy observed at the time that people were sacrificed to his poetry, 'to keep the flame burning. It is a Jamesian subject, I guess'. To most friends Lowell's behaviour was a second betrayal: Stanley Kunitz ('There are details which seem to me monstrously heartless'), Elizabeth Bishop ('art just isn't worth that much'). Adrienne Rich savaged the published book in review ('bullshit eloquence, a poor excuse for a cruel and shallow book'). Lowell substantially ignored Bishop's wonderfully supportive yet carefully reasoned letter of March 21st 1972 though he recognised it, as he wrote to Bidart, as 'a kind of masterpiece of criticism'. To him it seemed as much a technical as an ethical problem:

> I could say the letters are cut, doctored part fiction; I thought of it (I attribute things to Lizzie I made up, or that were said by someone else. I combed out abuse, hysteria, repetition.) The trouble is the letters make the book, I think, at least they make Lizzie real beyond my invention. I took out the worst things written against me, so as not to give myself a case and seem self-pitying.

Whether it is Lowell's Hardwick as Hardwick's own voice, the reader cannot but sympathise with her. In 'Hospital 11' he writes:

> You left two houses and two thousand books,
> a workbarn by the ocean, and two slaves
> to kneel and wait upon you hand and foot –
> tell us why in the name of Jesus.

Although this is apparently a reference to an August 1970 letter in which Hardwick listed some of the things he would miss by not returning (apartment, workbarn, friends) her words do not correlate with those in the poem and the 'slaves' comes from another context. Almost broken-hearted in 'Records', Lowell ventriloquizes Hardwick again, envisaging his future as an equivalent of her own past:

> you doomed to know what I have known with you,
> lying with someone fighting unreality –
> love vanquished by his mysterious carelessness.

The Dolphin is nominally a celebration of the mythologized Blackwood. Re-reading it I begin to wonder, though, how much room it has to express the wonder of this new love. There is awe and there is joy, but these are compromised by the break-up of the old marriage, new responsibilities and an alien life. The undertone can be heard in 'Flight to New York':

> After fifty so much joy has come,
> I hardly want to hide my nakedness –
> the shine and stiffness of a new suit, a feeling,
> not wholly happy, of having been reborn.

Worst is the crippling indecision. Lowell sees himself as Hamlet in one poem. In 'On the End of the Phone' it is his hypocrisy rankles. In 'Doubt' he names his problem: 'From the dismay of my old world to the blank / new – water-torture of vacillation!' In his confusion poems often recount dreams or move like dreams. There is a plethora of rhetorical questions ('What shall I do with my stormy life blown towards evening?'). The poet is lost beyond wonder ('If I cannot love myself, can you?') and fears for his adopted family of Blackwood and her three little girls ('how do I know I can keep any of us alive?'). In another poem, he wakes into tears.

All these concerns are contained within a plot, as Hamilton reminds us in her introduction to *The Dolphin: Two Versions*: 'He thinks of his pursuit of Caroline and of his own art as continuous.' We are dealing with an element of fiction, a tidying of fact. In 'Dolphin' he refers to 'this book, half fiction' and in 'Marriage' he has this to say:

> Ours was never a book, though sparks of it
> spotted the page with superficial burns:
> the fiction I colored with first-hand evidence,
> letters and talk I marketed as fiction

In her preface to *American Fictions* (1999) Hardwick quoted Ivy Compton-Burnett on finding real life no help to a writer because it has no plot. Here the poet constructs one. He falls in love, undergoes a manic episode, leaves hospital, vacillates, flies to New York to see his current wife, then makes a choice and remarries. Somewhere in there he and his new companion have a baby. In the first version (the manuscript circulated to friends) the baby's arrival comes at the end, in the published version earlier, where it helps to clarify his thinking.

The published versions of key poems like 'Fishnet' and 'Dolphin' are clearly superior and most readers would be satisfied with this 1973 collection – its notoriety aside – since there is a limit to one's willingness to keep attending to earlier versions. Interestingly though, in the manuscript of the title poem Lowell asks compassion for the book – a Shakespearean touch – whereas in published form, since 'my eyes have seen what my hand did', he now asks no compassion for his behaviour.

The Dolphin Letters offers at least some. Firstly we witness Hardwick's fortitude in the face of pain, humiliation and financial chaos resulting from their break-up – despite occasional explosions of bitterness. (The hysteria, having been 'combed out' of the poems, must have been mostly edited out of the letters at some point, if Hardwick were to be believed when she told Ian Hamilton that she wrote lengthy vitriolic ones at the time.) Lowell too emerges with some eloquence and conscience, despite his wilful blindness. (To Hardwick he writes on one occasion 'you couldn't have been more loyal and witty. I can't give you anything of equal value'. 'Not having you,' he writes in another letter, 'is like learning to walk.')

Since both were professional writers we should not be surprised at how intellectually vibrant and cultured each can be, even in distress, witty too. In the early letters we are reminded also of their busyness ('The phone rings all day with meetings one could attend, plays one is urged to go to in the freezing night, an occasional unwanted invitation, malignant growths of mail, bills'). We learn of the liberal commitment of both Lowells during the Vietnam and Nixon years. There is also a deal of agonising over money, taxes, selling Lowell's papers, Harriet's education and state of mind, all of which fell to Hardwick in his absence. Also there is room for good old gossip ('character analysis' as Hardwick liked to call it) and insights into social and political conditions in England.

Emotionally, however, the early letters make excruciating reading: Hardwick's excitement at the prospect of joining Lowell in England with their daughter; the knowledge that her loving notes inspire his uncharacteristic reticence; the inevitable leaking of the news of an affair; the realization that this is not the usual brief infidelity. In a prolonged series of exchanges Lowell is clearly ambivalent about both relationships ('one man, two women, the common novel plot', as he ruefully describes it in 'Exorcism') and vacillates chronically. Blackwood, being mostly at his side, rarely makes a direct appearance. Though he would love her to his death, the poem 'Caroline' reads like their epitaph:

Marriage? That's another story. We saw
the diamond glare of morning on the tar.
For a minute had the road as if we owned it.

There is a great deal of suffering. Time passes. Hardwick finally accepts the near-inevitable, focusing on the welfare of their daughter and resumes her own work, her writing and teaching. Slowly the two find another level for their relationship built on the foundations of the years of their marriage. The arrival of Lowell and Blackwood's baby, Sheridan, breaks the uneasy peace. Then, with divorce, Lowell is upset at the 'barracuda settlement' (the loss of the house in Castine, Maine, they had inherited, plus his trust fund). It is publication of *The Dolphin* that does most harm. Though Lowell assured her she would not 'feel betrayed or exploited' by it, that is exactly how Hardwick felt, especially after the review by Marjorie Perloff in *New Republic*, which is a scathing indictment of Lowell's 'taste' and his wife *and* daughter who 'seem to get no more than they deserve'.

Hardwick does not write for months. Eventually a new note enters the renewed correspondence: concern about Lowell's increasingly poor health. In December 1975 she describes to McCarthy his premature ageing and news of his turn to acupuncture from lithium. There is a measure of harmony, following regret on his part for the use of her letters. He writes his last and poignant collection, *Day By Day* ('Autobiography predominates, almost forty years of it. And now more journey of the soul'). Finally, with seemingly terminal problems in Lowell's relationship with Blackwood (fears relating to his mania and to her drinking) he reluctantly leaves her. He returns to the apartment at West 67th Street and Hardwick, where they achieve a comradeship. As Hardwick explains in mid-June 1977, 'We, together, are having a perfectly nice time, both quite independent and yet I guess dependent'. Three months later Lowell died.

I have been reading the poetry of Robert Lowell and his life story for forty years (and writing on him periodically for half that time), so I am in no position to complain about intrusion. Having said that, the fact that the focus of *The Dolphin Letters* is on a brief few dramatic years of Lowell's life – and not his finest – means that the glare of the letters seems greater. True the book dramatizes the issue of the boundaries of art and illustrates the trials of composition. Yet these letters are shockingly intimate, if not in a prurient sense. Our only defence is to remind ourselves that the authors, in effect, sold their stories. To Hardwick it would all be a dire 'appropriation' nevertheless: 'I can't tell you how I dread the future with biographies and Lizzie; to say nothing of "Cal" who will never be even touched with the truth of his own being and nature...It is such a violation, like a wound.'

Still there is something Lowell-like in the thought that for those of us who remain enthralled by the work of one of the great American poets of the twentieth century and one of its finest essayists, *The Dolphin* and *The Dolphin Letters* – once published – are inescapable.

Moving Day and other poems

JENNY KING

Were there Trams in Odessa?

(overheard question)

Sepia. Tall house-fronts, pale above the dark streets.
Three tiny figures in heavy coats,
walking. What year is it?

It is the sepia year of long ago.
There was no time then. Streets were empty,
shops unvisited.

Inscrutable stillness, the camera's moment
fixed against the flickering human eye.
Caged in history.

No. The picture's imagined, conjured up
by that creative tool the hopeful brain
which mixes memory and invention.

But such a place and such a year existed
outside the mind's embroidery. There was trade,
there were marriages,

as in the nameless photographs which drop
out of an album from your mother's youth –

But then of course they knew if there were trams.
An easy question.

Moving Day

One, two, three
　　　and we vault
　　　　　across the valley and land

here in another postcode
where a squirrel fossicks in the rain
on the moss-lumpy roof of now our garage
and the back of my mind says
when we get home
but we are home.

We wake to a mild, damp day
and walls of boxes. Oddments which can't be returned
to drawers which are ours no longer.
The unencumbered squirrel sits on its haunches
and enjoys the air.

We are in the sky,
living among treetops in the region
fir cones drop from. Out of the window
we sense the passing traffic of radio waves.

The future crouching in the valley
opens its arms as the sun rises and the row of pines
retract their shadows and whisper of possibilities.
We empty and stow, fight through our box walls like prisoners
digging a way out. Evening comes.

Morning comes, the fifth day. Birds look in at us
from their neighbourly branches. We are here
for keeps. Day passes. Far down the valley
an owl couches his soft notes on silence.

Goat

Old goat, two inches high,
carved from some dark wood in a Swiss valley
seventy years ago,
the painted bell on your neck still sounds
for your first owner and all the dead.

This morning as I lift you from beside my cow
I see your udder, plain as day.
How did I never notice in all these years?
Did I assume, because you were my brother's
who was older, stronger, that you were male?

Did I suppose that being male
gave him power beyond what I could hope for?
Fifteen years since he died.

Now I have passed his age. I hold his toy
as though an amulet against forgetting

and feel the decades flowing through my fingers
like water pouring down the cascade at Chatsworth
that makes its way patiently, out of sight,
then bursts from the heart of the lake
and moistens the air with its tall plume.

But looking from my window at the world
I think how sisters have biased opinions
and how I never understood that sometimes
memory's not a wisp of falling water
but a small, unexpected, solid thing.

Two Poems

LAURA SCOTT

The Wrong Man

It was in a Chinese restaurant. We were eating seaweed, first time I'd had it,
first time I'd been on my own with godfather and he was talking on and on
in a voice that never drew breath, a voice that unscrolled itself like one of those
proclamations with handles someone holds in a film and then drops so we see it
unrolling down the stairs. He was laying out the case, telling me how he ended up with
the wrong man, wrong colour hair, wrong eyes, wrong everything and I'm fourteen maybe
fifteen, sitting across the table from him trying to balance ivory chopsticks on the sides
of my fingers and stop the napkin sliding off my lap, not knowing what to say because
the thing is, I loved this wrong man more than the confiding godfather, especially the wave
in his hair, the way he smells expensive and his slightly plummy voice with a half-laugh in it
as if there's a joke stuck permanently in the back of his throat. There have been lots more
since then of course but only one who rhymed with him. Years later, different restaurant,
Italian this time, lots of people around a big table, after my father's funeral
and I'm talking to an aunt, the youngest and sweetest of his sisters who's telling me
of the man she should have married. And as she talks her voice holds him up like a waiter
bending back his wrist to carry a plate of oysters, shimmying through the spaces between
the tables until I see him, this talked of man, handsome, holding court in her bedroom,
his long legs stretched out, ankles balanced on the edge of her desk before I look up and see
my uncle watching us from the other side of the table, his unblinking eyes listening and
watering in the slab of his face, a white expanse of cloth between us. My poor uncle.

Lines

All these lines to remember, all these lines you'll forget –
the lines of birds forming and breaking,

breaking and forming, breathing in an imperfect V
across the sky. And the lines that crease

our palms, blown across our hands, heart lines, life lines,
folding and deepening, starring and intersecting,

lines the palmist longs to see. And the lines that fissure
and suture the skull, fusing plates of bone

together to shield the yolk of brain. Rilke dreamt
of playing them, of running a needle

across their groove so he could hear those wavering lines
scratch out their truth. All those lines

meandering, drawn by the same thing, all those lines
to remember, all those lines to forget.

Biala in Provincetown

MARY MAXWELL

TWO SUMMERS AGO Ford Madox Ford sat in the windowed front gallery of the Provincetown Art Association and Museum. Or rather, it was Janice Biala's painted image of him (*Portrait d'un Écrivain*, 1938) that seemed to ponder the late-summer comings and goings of the town's Commercial Street. I suspect that most visitors to *Biala: Provincetown Summers* were confused as to what exactly Ford was doing there, his peach and blue form awkwardly seated among her abstracted street scenes, interiors and seascapes.

For those familiar with Cape Cod art history, Janice Biala is primarily known as the sister of the artist Jack Tworkov. The pair had first come from New York City together in 1923 to study with Charles Hawthorne and his traditional *plein-air* approaches. Both quickly turned to other more experimental teachers. It was with Edwin 'Dick' Dickinson, Janice said, that she 'found her true way'. Biala, like Dickinson, was from the start a 'modernist'. This designation was made official by the Provincetown Art Association's 1927 'First Modernist Exhibition' in which Biala's earliest works were included. From the perspective of her future career, there is something distinctly prophetic in the show's title; only three years later Biala would be off to the continent.

In Paris Biala was almost immediately introduced to Ford and his circle of high modernist cohorts. Ford, of course, had for nearly two decades served as mentor and senior colleague to Pound, Williams and Stein, among many others. And it was through Ford and his circle that Biala encountered most intensively the European modernism (and later the persons) of Matisse, Picasso and Brancusi. Their nine-year love affair, a marriage in everything but legal technicality, was described by Biala as 'a long passionate dialogue'. At the time of Ford's death in 1939, Biala stayed on in Hitler-threatened France, making sure that Ford's library and manuscripts would be removed to safety in New York. In the summer of 1940, the year after Ford's death, she returned to the States to stay with the Dickinsons on Wellfleet's bayside. Period photographs show the feisty young widow, cigarette in hand, scouring the ocean's horizon or contemplating beach sand patternings. Dickinson's 1940 *Janice at the Beach* (unfortunately not included in the PAAM show) captures the tear-blurred beauty of her grieving. There's only one Biala work in the PAAM show dating from this period, a small pencil drawing of shacks perched high on a dune. Curator Jason Andrews writes that it 'seems to reflect the solitary and emotional turmoil Biala must have been enduring at the loss of Ford', though the apparent lack of work from the summer perhaps suggests even more about her bereft mental state.

By 1942 Biala had married the French artist Daniel Brustlein (who made his living as 'Alain', a cartoonist for *The New Yorker*); for the following decades their lives alternated between New York and Paris. Dickinson's journal records a 1943 dinner at the Brustleins, spent in the company of Willem and Elaine de Kooning. The newly married pair of Brustlein and Biala were among de Kooning's earliest collectors; in fact, Biala arranged the modest wedding lunch for Elaine and Willem. In 1949 the DeKoonings spent the month of July in Provincetown (whose idea would likely have been either Janice or Jack's), though apparently the couple did more partying than painting. That same year Elaine wrote about Dickinson for *Art News*: 'The poetic content' she observed 'is an important part of the expression.'

In 1958 Biala's brother Jack bought a house in Provincetown's West End. By then the postwar Outer Cape had attracted a new group of New York bohemians, many of them wartime émigrés from Europe. Like previous generations drawn by its particular light, there remained in the country's 'first arts colony' a quality nearly as European as the bookshelves of its summer intelligentsia. (During the McCarthy era, the community's social and political liberality continued to be decidedly 'un-American'.) Provincetown scenes from this period in the PAAM show include several collages (*Provincetown* and *Le* (sic) *Grande Plage* (humorously mistranslated as 'the grand beach') both from 1957. Unsurprisingly, after her brother bought his house on Commercial Street (the show includes several photographs of Janice on its porch), the presence of Cape Cod becomes more evident (*Hillside*, 1958 and *The Beach,* 1958). In 1959 a show at Provincetown's HCE Gallery exhibited Biala's work alongside her brother and Dickinson. Dore Ashton wrote, 'In several of her best paintings, Biala keeps to the tonal palette the Cape Cod ambiance demands, using it with great finesse'.

Even when the result is figurative, Biala approaches the canvas much as an abstractionist would. Her dislike of Hawthorne's 'plein air' stemmed not from any dislike of the outdoors; it was just that reproduction of the immediate didn't interest her. Her paintings' 'subject' was experience, an imaginative product of both immediate and recalled perception. And so any assertion that works such as her 1958 *Hillside* or *Beach* mark some kind of rejection of the 'male-dominated era of New York School of Abstract Expressionism' (as Andrews describes it) is disproven by such works themselves. In my view, *Beach* can nearly be read as an homage to de Kooning. Biala surely would have heard about the painter's drunken afternoon on a Provincetown beach back in 1949 (as recorded in the de Kooning Stevens/Swan biography), an escapade in which he and two friends found themselves naked in a very stormy surf, ending up in jail for 'resisting arrest' and 'indecent exposure'. Writes de Kooning's biographers: 'The powerful sensations aroused in him by the sea... entered his work that summer as a kind of brief counterpoint to the dark, existential brooding of his gritty urban paintings.' So, too, Biala's passionate and powerful red, white and blue *Beach* shows she was also fully capable of de Kooningesque muscular gesturalism. And, I would infer from the painting, Biala had her eye on now-better-known female American contemporaries working in abstraction such as Krasner, Hartigan, and Frankenthaler.

What I perceive as her strongest Cape work results from such vocational interactions and engagements. As John Ashbery observed of a 1961 group show in Paris: 'The finest painting in the show is easily [...] by Janice Biala, which uses abstract and figurative techniques to piece together a remarkably complete portrait that exists on several levels – as painting, as an impression of physical truth, as a perception of the world of the spirit.' This 'neo-impresssionism' particularly expresses itself in the Cape landscapes from the mid-sixties, works in the PAAM show such as *Provincetown Harbor*, 1963; *Newcomb Hollow, Wellfleet*, 1965; *Long Point*, 1967; and *Arbe et la Mer: Provincetown*, 1967. This last work is of special interest, as it presents not an actual perception; objectively, Provincetown's Pilgrim Monument is shown too large to be an accurate view from Wellfleet or even Truro's bayside (where it was more likely to have been painted, despite its catalogue identification). Instead it is a composite memory, part Cape and part South of France.

Perhaps in this sense, the figure of Ford in the show is not so out of place after all. Certainly what the great writer believed about literary creation could equally apply to the deeply psychological approaches of Dickinson: 'The seen distortion is what the thought did to the sight.' This is, as it happens, very Fordian. In fact, what John Ashbery has written of Dickinson could be applied to certain approaches of Ford: 'The problem of painting 'from life' with total accuracy and honesty involves lies and distortions.' In terms of surface as well, Ford and Dickinson are very alike in that in both their works, something is always a bit skewed; narrative perspective lacks fixity (is 'unreliable'), leaving the reader/observer with a sensation of distinctive off-balance. The subject of a painting is not the object itself but rather the terms of its perception. Or as Biala quotes Ford, 'Only states of mind count'.

Of course, my response to *Provincetown Summers* is colored by my own interactions with the lives and works of Ford and Biala, as well as by my personal familiarity with the Outer Cape. And so, as grateful as I am for the show's existence, I came away with a set of strong reservations. The first of these was its failure to explain her as a 'Provincetown painter', most especially in her relation to Dickinson but also to Provincetown's artistic community. Secondly, as I've suggested, her and Dickinson's relationship to de Kooning is too important to leave out – and not just as a biographical detail but as an element of American art history. Certainly it's a crucial element of Biala's relation to the New York School. Finally, it was immensely frustrating that there was no real catalogue containing considered analysis of her time in Provincetown by a person well informed about the Outer Cape. As a result of overlooked or mistakenly identified persons, artifacts and locations (as just one example, the show places the Dickinson household in neighboring Truro), *Provincetown Summers* was a lost opportunity to present Biala as a significant presence in mid-century cultural life. At the very least, Biala stands as a common link between three important postwar modernist 'moments' in Paris, New York and Provincetown. In a letter to her brother, Janice had written: 'Creating a great painter is not only a question of being a great painter – it is a thing that is achieved by a number of factors working together for that end.' Particularly if 'greatness' stems from influential personal connections, the career of Biala demands serious reconsideration.

Biala: Provincetown Summers, selected paintings and drawings was at the Provincetown Art Association and Museum, August 10-September 30, 2018, curated, with an online catalogue by, Jason Andrew, available for free download at: https://www.janicebiala.org/solo-exhibitions

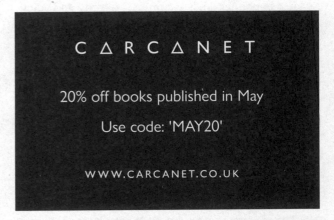

Three Poems

CAROL RUMENS

Variations for W.S. Graham on the 100th centenary of his birth

I have made myself alone now.
Outside the tent endless
Drifting hummock crests.
Words drifting on words.
The real unabstract snow.
W.S. Graham,
'Malcolm Mooney's Land'

What everyone thinks, I
suppose, who has time
to form thought-like
shapes during the long
plunge into the crevasse;
many, all their lives,
have traipsed towards it,
equipped but unprepared
ever to hear it holler:
I have made myself alone now.

The only paradise
is motion, lost
to encampment, both
improvised. Sometimes
the bed must be unfolded
still warm from under us,
torn for another sail;
on the plate, the bleak dog-meat,
outside the tent endless
drifting hummock crests.

Bodies row their own
furrows, wry channels,
other breathers always
just out of earshot.
Now and again the mouth
makes kissing-sounds.
The pack (the pawed god
of the team) will quicken now,
mapping the maps, fresh
words drifting on words.

You know where I'm going
with this. Of course.
It's January, the coarse-
gritted wind of a hundred
Januaries hurtles
from your mound. Yr Wyddfa freckles
with treacherous blackthorn.
High-skilled for the gradient
you're gracing it through
the real unabstract snow.

To Gwynedd

'Meseems I see the high and stately mountains
Transform themselves to low dejected valleys'.
'Ye Goatherd Gods', Philip Sidney

Land of our grandmother, Alys Emily!
Land not entirely unambiguous
in welcome, creasy grin a kind of judgement,
you're so old you're young – wild teenager,
harddegau gwyllt –
your slept-in look eternally morning-after-
the-mountain-rave, petrified evidence
of ruckus, rape and knife-fight. Slumped in riverine
spillage, they who love you
might wake up poets   if they wake up.

Strung out on bright blue lakes
we take the hairpin bends too
Jesus   too
fa   slow down! Volcano madness, this is!
They'll kick us soon as look. I hardly see them
for seeing our bones cheese-sandwiched in the landbits
we owned, whose cast-off selves owned all of it
and reasoned, 'Let the Welshman break the stone'.

Payback-seductress, summer Gwynedd fleeces
the fleecy-lined colonists from Chester
and Merseyside and Moscow with
Llanfairpwllgwyngyllgogerychwyrndrobwllllantysiliogogogoch,
with pretty inn-signs, warmish beer, sogged fries.
She drains the thirsty drop-outs from all over,
to her sale of mushroom-magic, yurty glamping,
the rock 'n' roll of waterfall and runoff.
Old music-mouth, old gossip, mocker, peace-

offering your ironic cartoon dragon
to Grendel's fossil claws,
Gwynedd, don't be angry!
Our shiny notes are bankable, at least.
Don't die to us. Let's end our letters only
as Alys Emily Davies, gifted in
the paler dragon's tongue, would temporise
in the blue shadow of her mountain ranges,
'Must close for now, dear. Yrs affectionately...'

(Stanza 3, line 4, the Angelsey place-name translates as 'St Mary's church in the
hollow of the white hazel near to the fierce whirlpool of St Tysilio of the red cave')

A Wooden Swing

(Variations on Osip Mandelstam's 'Tolka chitat...')

1. Upswing

To read only children's stories,
Cultivate little ideas,
And rub away the tears
Of adult categories...

Life? It's a rouble's-worth,
But here's the thing –
I want to sing and sing
My poor, rich, singular earth.

A garden, a child's swing –
I'm flying on the bare
Plank, king of the fir,
through this wild darkening.

2. Downswing

Never to answer emails;
To read kind horoscopes
Only, and let the snails
Chew my envelopes...

What a waste of a good idea,
Childhood was! Light kills
Both snow and clay's career:
Why all these daffodils?

We made a swing for our hopes
On a branch long overgrown.
They've kicked the nettles down.
They jeer from weathered ropes.

Unstated Empson

Looking for Traces of the Chinese Poetic Tradition

DIANA BRIDGE

'twittering ghosts'

Months ago, reading a review of William Empson's *The Face of the Buddha* in the pages of this magazine (PNR 232), my eye was caught by an excerpt from the book that should have been Empson's third but was eventually published seventy years after it was completed. Empson wrote of a ceramic luohan (saint or sage in the Buddhist pantheon) observed at the Royal Academy in 1935, that the figure 'seemed...so much alive that it turned the people looking at it in the London Exhibition into twittering ghosts'. In his review, Mark Thompson suggested that Eliot's 'twittering world' stood behind Empson's response and connected it to the language and ambience of *Burnt Norton*. Empson's China background brings up a possible additional source.

Empson used the arresting phrase when revising the manuscript of his book in the 1940s, after his return from China. He had spent the years 1937-1939 teaching English literature at National Peking University, when the war with Japan had necessitated the university's relocation to Changsha and Kunming. Empson had taught in gruelling conditions and mostly from memory. It was his prodigious memory that made me wonder whether the combination of ghosts and twittering might have had a relationship, direct or subterranean, with the last two lines of the Tang poet Du Fu's famous poem, 'Ballad of the Army Carts'. In the prose translation by Empson's friend David Hawkes, these lines read: 'The new ghosts complain and the old ghosts weep, and under the grey and dripping sky the air is full of their baleful twitterings' (*A Little Primer of Tu Fu*, OUP 1967).

It was, and still is, common Chinese practice to recite poems from memory. Empson's own Chinese was less than slight but there must have been times when he heard famous Chinese poems recited and translated for his benefit by the English speakers among his colleagues.[1] In the situation in which the university was placed, in retreat from the advancing Japanese, 'Ballad of the Army Carts' would not have been an improbable choice of poem.

Du Fu's ballad depicts the personal and social costs that arose from conscripting the peasantry into military service. It culminates in the conscripted men's bones being left to lie in the desert wastes beyond their homeland. Hawkes's addition of 'baleful' to 'twitterings' reflects the extremity of such a fate. Whether Empson heard the poem spoken aloud and translated in this way we don't know; nor, if he did, can we be sure of how the last lines were rendered. Nonetheless, there is not a lot of scope for translating *gui*, ghost. The reduplicated character *jiu jiu*, twittering, can also mean chirping but, in this context, chirping can be firmly ruled out.

These thoughts were overtaken by the arrival of the following lines from Matthew Arnold's narrative poem 'Balder Dead':[2]

> And from the dark flock'd up the shadowy tribes:
> And as the swallows crowd the bulrush-beds
> Of some clear river, issuing from a lake,
> On autumn days, before they cross the sea;
> And to each bulrush-crest a swallow hangs
> Swinging, and others skim the river streams,
> And their quick twittering fills the banks and shores –
> So around Hermod swarm'd the twittering ghosts.

Along with the linguistic concurrence, the telling antithesis implanted in Empson's description would seem to follow Arnold. I cannot shake off the possibility that Du Fu's translated poem came Empson's way, fused in his mind with Arnold's eerie Homeric simile and returned to invigorate his criticism. It seems significant that when he employed the description it was in the context of an exhibition of Chinese art:

'Most wrecked and longest of all histories'

For an idea of the way in which Empson's mind synthesised material, looked at through the prism of his Chinese subject matter, I turned to his three 'China poems'. The first two were written during his initial stint in the country and the third in 1951, when he was again teaching at Peking University under the auspices of the British Council. 'China', written in early 1938, draws on standard versions of Chinese mythology, history and culture. The life of the poem lies in the fusion of these gleanings with Empson's vivid on the ground observations – most strikingly, 'the paddy-fields are wings of bees'; and its boldness from the way in which they are subordinated to two conceits. 'The dragon hatched a cockatrice', drawn from Isaiah, works from the observation that many features of Japanese culture were absorbed from Tang dynasty China. China is of course the dragon.

Empson next employs the metaphor of a liver fluke merging so completely with its host that it becomes one with it to comment zanily on the idea that China has been able to absorb and sinicize all her invaders.[3] Living through it, he believes that eventually she will do the same with the Japanese. It matters not at all that he has got the host and the type of liver fluke wrong. It is the pertinent analogy for seamless assimilation that counts. The summary in the poem's final line, 'Most wrecked and longest of all histories', holds a challenging ironic balance worthy of Empson:

'what / In God's name are you doing here?'

'China' might be the outcome of early encounter but it is wide-ranging, confident and at home with its Chinese material. The long poem 'Autumn on Nan-Yuëh', written in 1938–39 when the military situation was looking less positive and the 'temporary university' on the brink of relocating to Kunming, reads quite differently. Deftly applied cultural stereotype gives way to a personal and in places painfully reflective, verse. The tone, though, is light, that of rueful raconteur.

The epigraph to the poem is telescoped Yeats, taken from 'The Phases of the Moon'. Empson finds a bizarre correlative for Yeats' visionary repertoire in the hideously disabled pilgrims he saw being helped or winched up Nan Yue, a mountain sacred to Taoism and itself traditionally regarded as sacred. The poem is structured by a Yeatsian vocabulary of 'flight', 'cradle', 'deformed' and 'dream' as a deeply assimilated poem from his own tradition provides the architecture for one of Empson's own.

'Autumn on Nan-Yűeh' mingles topical political with cultural observation. Allusions range from the Bible to Freud, Woolf to Alice. But those who 'can use Chinese', as Empson put it in *Seven Types of Ambiguity*, bring another awareness to bear. The English poet's role as scholar-literatus, his immediate predicament, and his response to it, which is to write, are features that might place him in the long ribbon of Chinese poets despatched on service, or banished, from the centre. The response of those poets was to describe their exotic rural surroundings and to interrogate their own situation. I am unable to find in the poem, or its notes, a pointer to any Chinese poem or poet, and yet its concerns chime with those that preoccupy the Chinese scholar-poet, separation, exile or escape, questioning the value of the path that one has chosen, loneliness and loss.[4]

Could the similarity be intended or are we looking at a common human response to dislocation and privation? On the side of the first interpretation is the fact that Empson had reviewed Arthur Waley's *Poems from the Chinese* (Benn, 1927), a selection from Waley's three previous books of translations, for the Cambridge magazine *The Granta* (November 4, 1927). It is not fanciful to think of his reading Waley's other seminal translations from the Chinese which, together, provide an idea of the Chinese poet's themes over a millennium. Nor does it seem far-fetched to conceive of Empson allowing one of his own poems that closely connects to those concerns to run alongside the Chinese tradition in sprightly foreign parallel.

In his first book, *Seven Types of Ambiguity*, written several years before he went to China, Empson had drawn on Waley's translation of a poem by Tao Qian (365-427CE): 'Swiftly the years, beyond recall./Solemn the stillness of this spring morning.'[5] Using the lines as an example, he offered a radiantly expressed and sure summing up of the use of contrasted time-scales and, in the process, revealed an understanding of the thinking that underlies the structuring of many an early Chinese poem. 'Both these time-scales and their contrasts are included by these two lines in a single act of apprehension, because of the words swift and still. Being contradictory as they stand, they demand to be conceived in different ways; we are enabled, therefore, to meet the open skies with an answering stability of self-knowledge; to meet the brevity of human life with an ironical sense that it is morning and spring time, that there is a whole summer before winter, a whole day before night.'

For a moment I indulge the thought that Tao Qian, who both accommodates a pedigree of allusion in his poems and is acclaimed for his genius for plain expression, is the Chinese poet closest to Empson. A further link would be hard to pass over. In *A hundred and seventy*

Chinese Poems (Constable, 1918), a contributor volume to *Poems*, I count in the twelve poems by Tao ten mentions of the joys of drinking wine, these lines among them: 'Idly I drink at the eastern window. / Longingly – I think of my friends.' Empson is likely to have felt an affinity with that recurring topos. Without doubt he would have heard his colleagues talk about the link between drinking and poetic composition. Is it incidental that he devotes a whole stanza of 'Autumn' to a better-than-expected 'Tiger Bone' beer, used by 'The chaps... for getting near'?

'it is true I flew, I fled'

The theme of flight pervades the stanzas of 'Autumn'. The Japanese planes preparing to strafe the railway lines of the nearby town are just its most up-to-date and literal embodiment. As an aspiration to escape a difficult earthbound life, flight is present from early times in Chinese lyric poetry. Often it is expressed as the wish to become a bird. The concluding couplet of the fifth 'Old Poem', composed around the second century CE and itself drawing on an old song, concludes, 'She wants to become those two wild geese / That with beating wings rise high aloft' (*A hundred and seventy Chinese Poems*, 13). In his escape from 'They / Who sat on pedestals and fussed', Empson had become a wild goose. Now he 'who said [he] wouldn't fly again / For quite a bit' was in the process of fleeing once more.

High Traditions

In a note to 'China', Empson speaks, not for the only time, of 'the separation of the beauty of the coolie life (the reference here is to singing) from the official arts'. This is followed by the observation: 'The paddy fields in hill country... seem never to have been treated by all the long and great tradition of Far Eastern landscape painters.' Sentiments like these might at least partly explain why he did not engage directly with that 'official art', the classical poetry tradition. It was a different matter a few years later when it came to art inspired by Communist ideals and objectives, and to the last of Empson's 'China' poems.

'So your flesh shall be part of mine
And part of mine be yours.'

Empson's unwavering feeling for China and its people, his own ideological orientation and his lived experience come together in 'Chinese Ballad'. Composed in 1951, this is a translation of a section of a long narrative poem by Li Ji, a political instructor in the People's Liberation Army who, in the course of his duties, gathered Shanxi folksongs, using one as the basis for a long work of his own. Empson had been made aware, probably by David Hawkes, of the existence of a pedigree for the passage. In his notes he attributes the original lines to the calligrapher and painter Zhao Mengfu (1254–1322), one of the Four Great Masters of the Yuan Dynasty, whom he refers to as a 'poet'.

For something closer to the full story we need to jump to a review of Empson's poem by David Hawkes.[6] Hawkes relates an anecdote about Zhao who, late in a happy marriage, advised his wife, Guan Daosheng, that he was about to take a concubine. Lady Guan, herself a talented painter, calligrapher and poet, provided a sophisticated remonstrance in the form of this poem.[7] It seems that she won the day. Hawkes's research into the linguistic background reveals that the language of this portion of Li Ji's ballad ties it to the area from which the couple came. This was also the region where the clay figures to which the ballad alludes were widely produced, which seems to clinch the attribution. The twists and turns of Hawkes's narrative, as he relays it in the article, and as he believed he might have conveyed it in part to Empson in Peking, provides fascinating context. But the detail does not make much difference to Empson's version.

Empson relates that he was told the meaning of the Chinese characters and that he translated word for word, with one exception – he introduced children alongside the word for doll, on the grounds that the term specifically means 'dolls for children'.[8] The apparent ease with which the Chinese folk song, with its repetitions, rhyme and simple poignant language, is converted into the world of the English ballad, and the way in which that world is underpinned by Empson's robust blend of English ballad rhythms, almost convinces you that there is such a thing as 'world ballad style'.[9]

John Donne was one of Empson's favourite poets and the translation also exudes echoes of 'The Good-Morrow' and 'A Valediction: Forbidding Mourning'. These refined echoes recall the Chinese ballad's sophisticated genesis. They offer indirect support to Empson's comment that 'it is very fine metaphysical poetry at the end, when the clumsy little doll is to wait, through all eternity, just for a few days'.

Now he has seen the girl Hsiang-Hsiang,
    Now back to the guerrilla band;
And she goes with him down the vale
    And pauses at the strand.

The mud is yellow, deep, and thick,
    And their feet stick, where the stream turns.
'Make me two models out of this,
    That clutches as it yearns.

'Make one of me and one of you,
    And both shall be alive.
Were there no magic in the dolls
    The children could not thrive.

'When you have made them smash them back:
    They yet shall live again.
Again make dolls of you and me
    But mix them grain by grain.

'So your flesh shall be part of mine
    And part of mine be yours.
Brother and sister we shall be
    Whose unity endures.

'Always the sister doll will cry,
    Made in these careful ways,
Cry on and on, Come back to me,
    Come back in a few days.'

Empson loved this poem. Its subject coalesces with 'the mud theme' flowing through his own work but here the magical qualities attributed to the mud lift it into a new dimension.[10] If 'Chinese Ballad' becomes the theme's apotheosis, it also comprises the most transparently human variation on a topic that first made its way to the surface in one of Empson's earliest poems with a description of the fertility of a land enriched by the practice of warping.

Taken together, the China-based poems inscribe a process of growing closeness between Empson and a culture that attracted him as a student and kept its hold on him as he experienced in person some of the most turbulent times in its history. The three poems replicate that process in terms of a poetic progress. Starting with a double conceit that lassoes interpretations of Chinese culture and history and presses them into service, following up with a personal account the themes of which parallel those of much Chinese poetry, it concludes with a response that is strong enough to leap the boundaries of language and allow the outsider to speak in the voice of a Chinese. The poems are like steps in a process of assimilation.

NOTES

1   'My colleagues habitually talked to each other in a jumble of three or four languages... using rather more English if they remembered I was listening; and of course a thorough understanding of Chinese literature would be taken for granted.' William Empson The Complete Poems, Penguin Classics 2001, p.387.

2   The lines, from 'An Episode. II. Journey to The Dead', were sent to me by Vincent O'Sullivan.

3   Later, when the military situation worsened and, by the middle of 1938, provoked a strong response from the desperate and beleaguered Chinese, Empson resiled from the passivity implicit in the metaphor.

4   I refer to excerpts from Empson's letters and introductions to his readings that appear as notes in the Collected Poems.

5   Empson has 'spring' for Waley's 'fair'; see 'New Corn' in Poems from the Chinese, 17.

6   Times Literary Supplement, 13 February, 2009, pp.13–15.

7   Hawkes advises that it was written in 'a racy contemporary vernacular with a trace of Jiangsu dialect in it' rather than the 'classical style', as Empson believed. In his inaugural lecture as Professor of Poetry at Oxford, delivered in 1961, Hawkes discussed this section of the ballad, which possessed a complicated history of colloquial text interwoven with classical explication. His aim was to impress on his audience the importance of offering both colloquial and classical Chinese to those who were to become his students. See Classical, Modern and Humane: Essays in Chinese Literature, ed. John Minford and Siu-kit Wong, The Chinese University Press, 1989, pp.13–14.

8   As Hawkes points out, the word niren used in the poem means doll in the sense of 'clay figure'. There is another term, niwawa, or niwa, that means clay dolls for children, and perhaps Empson's translator, whoever he was, drew on it when explaining the nuances of the poem. The Chinese and Empson's version are not identical. For a translation closer to the original, see Hawkes ibid.

9   In a 'Note by translator' above the poem as first published, Empson wrote that 'it seemed to me to fall into English ballad style as world ballad style'.

10 See also Mark Thompson's 'Mud & Blood' (PNR 235).

The Piano Tuner's Cough

GERARD WOODWARD

The tuner of our piano is making his final call,
And I am here to watch him work. His jacket's
Off and hanging from a chair. His sleeves
Are rolled like two white life-rings round each arm,
And in this way he strikes me as a working man –
A gardener come to tackle our wilderness,
A plumber trying to sort our drainage out.
He plays one note, then turns the tuning pin.
The piano is opened up, its strings exposed,
As if prepared for surgery, or strapped
To a chair, gagged or drugged or blacked out
Or fully conscious but with shredded nerves,
Like my mother at the dentist when her last few teeth
Were pulled, half cut with drink that made it
All the worse when her china-thin and sooted
Lower incisors snapped. He plays one note –
A half-truth, a near-truth, another turn and then

Another turn. He listens. The voice comes back
To him, barely a whisper. Telling him something
He already knows.

We are getting on okay. The tuner stands
My company, though looking back I see him
As a man in pain, ill at ease with kids.
His strongest wish is that I'd take my leave
And toddle off to my world of shrunken heads.
But he gives my questions their tired due and speaks
As if to someone older than myself
Which is a sort of compliment, but I
Do not understand a thing he says
And in between my questions are long rests
(Of a semibreve at least), in which I feel
No awkwardness and turn my ear instead
To the piano's slowly rising pleas for mercy.

The piano tuner coughs and from his mouth
A piece of silver jumps and lands on a spot
Of lacquered black just inches from my eyes,
To settle there a moment – barely a moment –
Before the tuner wipes the thing away
With the same soft cloth that gloves his tuning lever.
It is like a trick in which he's disappeared,
Leaving just a memory in his place
Though I still see the bubbled thing he'd wiped,
As if he'd coughed it straight into my thoughts –
awkwardness made visible; a little
Palace of the solecism, domed
And chambered, mirror-walled; pavilion
At an international exhibition;
Intersecting geodes; a jewel of
Buckminsterfullerene; short-lived hothouse
Seeded with more versions of himself,
His hereditary stuff, badge of how
Animal he really was, poor man.

Now I wonder if he was a father
With little angels seated at a different
Keyboard, generous with his time, loving,
Kind, but then that structure comes to mind,
The one he coughed, and through its curving glass
I see him as a tyrant who would rather
Cut his children's fingers off than hear them
Play a wayward note. Dr Harmonious,
Is he ill? Has he an ague?
Why this sudden vulnerability?
Is he sick of this tuning game,
And in his dreams sees armies of
Pianos with their bass strings drawn,
And elaborates his grand designs to turn them
Into other things? A reassembled
Fleet of sleek black galleons, for instance,
Their strings restrung as rigging. Or renailed
As garden sheds in which a quieter life
Can be pursued, seedlings raised in silence,
Noiseless pots of peaty soils tuned
By sunlight. Or might he snap completely
And take an axe to the reverberating wood
And find the other instrument I'm told
Is hidden there, that if you chopped away
The surrounding pine the structure that emerged
Would be something very like a harp
(It happens in a Marx Brothers film, I can't
Remember which one), as though it stored
The equipment for an afterlife, though some
Blackness in him sees his soul instead
Arrayed on red hot strings and hammered at
By hammers of burning lead. Tuner in torment.
No more false notes, no more half-truths,
The piano cries out in pain as he reaches
For its tongue and pulls it out, again.

A black cloud. A thunderhead. A stilted
Land. At two or three, a world above.
Its underneath to me seemed like a map
Of roads in an ideal city, intersections
And junctions of black wood that my matchbox cars
Could drive like they were in another land,
Suspended, antipodean – and whose feet are those,

In the upright world, treading so lightly, cautiously,
On the brass pedals, the same soft tread
My father's suede foot applied to the brake.
Then my mother, open-toed, overdoing the sostenuto.
At four or five another country came
Into view when I could see above the dark
Horizon - ploughed fields, but ploughed with a blade
Of pure exactness, and intersecting at
An angle – making overlapping slender
X's in three dimensions. An ocean,
An inland sea with waves unreally parallel
That turn their tides on golden breakwaters,
And come ashore on beaches of green baize
And a hundred capstans round which each string is moored.
The hump-backed bridges to nowhere, the dampers like molars
Chewing at the sound; in the bass more like incisors,
White felt v's that bite into the vibration
And silence it; the little gold leaf bunkers
Like a pharaoh's coffin that has been opened up
And found to be full of the ashes of burnt-out Woodbines.
The music rest with its black fret sunrise, the half moon
Rinks where cigarettes sometimes stood on end
In the place where a metronome once kept order. Time
Is not a tuner's concern, he plays the notes
Without a thought for a regular beat,
A musician from a universe that hasn't begun
Though with his keys turning and tightening
He can seem like a winder of clocks, just as he
Can seem anything – The priests who stopped
For sherry and a chat in those times
When our house was a place that could be visited,
The Provident man, the man who delivered our food.

It was his final call. He didn't come again.
And now the instrument is dying.
It is a wounded thing – don't let its size
Fool you, it is weak, lame, battle-scarred.
It is infected, it has rot rising from its golden feet,
I had thought he had come here to cure it but instead
He has given it an illness. This bronchial man
Is sick, there is something tapping at his heart,
Plucking at his own decaying strings. Perhaps he died.

And the piano lived on like an orphan in a fallen city,
A child whose frozen cot can't hold its warmth,
Whose voice drifts further and further from its human note.
You wouldn't treat an animal like that.

An observation blister on a futuristic craft,
The tuner within, peering out into a galaxy gone dark,
In mourning for his dying trade that once survived
On an instrument in every house. He had never seen
A grand like this, sitting in a room done up in white
(lino, walls and ceiling) the Bechstein of such polished
Black it was like a hole in time. He'd known it then,
Before its world fell in, with a gifted young musician
At its seat, and he could see perhaps the things
It had in store, and maybe this is what had made him sick.

Three Poems

ZOHAR ATKINS

Yom Kippur 2017

after Yehuda Amichai

On Yom Kippur, 2017, the year of DACA, I put on
my wedding *kittel* and walked through a city
that was neither old nor young.
For a long time, I stood in front of a poster
of the Old City of Jerusalem that was hanging
from a Chinatown bodega.
Outside Damascus Gate,
I could almost decipher a poet, dismounting
to confess a year's supply of regrets
to an Arab shopkeeper.
I lifted up my eyes to the corner
where a ram appeared, still and hornless,
afraid of its freedom.
The shop was full of shofars, dangling from the ceiling.
But deduction failed me.
Everything in sight was of antelope and oryx, blackbuck and addax.
Not a ram's horn to be found.
I searched until the light became so radiant I had to look away.
I couldn't stay to hear the poet's eloquence or its rebuttal.
I imagined ducks in the tears of both men,
swimming towards each other, hoping for
recognition.
When I finished, the time of the Closing of the Gates had passed.

Nineveh

An odd fact is that Jonah wanted to go to Nineveh.
It was on his bucket list.
He just didn't want to be a prophet.

As a student, he'd always dreamed
of visiting their fabled bakeries and libraries,
of observing the spectacular sacrifices to Baal.

In another life, he might even have fled *towards* Nineveh,
stuffed his ears with pitch and bitumen
and renounced the voices in his head.

But God had other plans,
and used Jonah,
making him doubly defiant,

a renunciate not only of divine commandment,
but of his own desire for a secular life.
As if it were the punch line to some dialectical joke

that can only be appreciated
by the depressive realists in heaven,
nothing could have been more pious

than boarding the ship to Tarsus.
It was by this sign that God knew Jonah
was prepared to convert the idolaters of the great city.

For the lesson of repentance that he needed
is that we must see our avoidance and our drive
as leading to the same place.

In the unedited version,
God shows Jonah that Nineveh was a Potemkin Village
made only for him:

The wicked foreigners
were copies of what he found distasteful in himself
and his own people.

An Israelite can never leave
his land, even if he calls it by a different name.
We children of Nineveh know this best:

No Torah, no 3,000 year history, no
prophecy or law can mute the voice
of heaven humming in our ears.

Elegy for a Special Kid

I.

I remember the day Isaac came into my classroom,
out of breath with excitement.
'I can't do tomorrow's homework –
I'm going to Mount Moriah!'
He flashed his father's illegible note.
There were many things that made him a special kid
His neck was shaped like a pill.
His head looked like an amulet.
His skin was translucent.

II.

'If the story of Isaac teaches us anything
it's that every knife is a compliment
and the greatest sacrifice of all is to throw it away.'
My analyst reads from his new book, *Isaac*
at the release party.
'To disregard evidence of our worth
in favor of a faith that it does not depend on being chosen –

for death as for recognition –
is to become more and less than a hero –
is to become free.'

I wonder how being named *Isaac* led him
to become a self-described *healer*
and whether the positive coverage will help or hurt him.

III.

I once read a Midrash
that Abraham offered Isaac the knife
and started to bind himself on the altar.
But the thought of killing his father was too much.
So Isaac removed the binding and placed himself in his stead.
This explains why there was no resistance. Why,
when Isaac got up, there were no bruises.
And why the ram seemed to die, of its own will
before the knife could fall.

Life-Cycle of the Herring Gull

HORATIO MORPURGO

dedicated to all who held Waterloo Bridge for Extinction Rebellion 15th – 21st April 2019

In the privacy of a side-street, off-season,
Two herring gulls are humping in the empty driveway
Of somebody's second home – and how
All of that seems only yesterday when

I step out one night to a whooshing
And a swooping feathered form from which
I flinch although it is only nature's way
To let me know they will once again be

Nesting on my neighbour's roof. From now on
That round-the-clock chimney-top look-out
Counts us in and out. There will be
Tight security around the first barbecue.

August again brings narrow coast-roads all a-glitter
With traffic tailed back for miles in the heat.
How their grey fuzzy young fill out, come quickly into focus
Just by waiting on soiled slates through long afternoons.

From the nervous glances you'd guess they hatch out
Fully advised of what the local paper says about their parents –
Bin-bag slashers and spreaders of our copious rubbish
All over the road! All over the beach!

Ice-cream snatchers! Shame on them! Reminders
Of so much we'd rather not know about the same sea
We adore on TV then fill to the brim with our trash.
They jeer at the sea-views for which we paid extra,

Shit on our cars and our weekend getaways,
Will smash and grab your toddler's portion of chips,
Down the lot and be sicking it up on my neighbour's roof
Even before the tears are dry down by the pier.

*

The moon is rising over a parched hill
And the voices of the young are flightless, stuck,
Grown squeaky with summer-long repetitions.
The cries of their parents are free-floating,

Moon-lit from above, street-lit from below,
But young or old, day or night, the combined clamour
Scrawls itself all over the sky like graffiti
Completely filling the underside of a railway arch.

The first-ever English book about birds has them
'Always querulous and full of noise'.
Four or five centuries on and the din is still describing
Great circles over the town and we are still

Respectable and shocked, as if
Hearing it for the first time.
When at a loss before the indecipherable, write
Dear Sir / Madam, urging extreme measures.

Cinquaines

Leo Boix

of Deal

MAN OF KENT

Upstairs
a bus to Deal
I'll beat the hell out of
you heard the Kentish lad. Scratched panes
fog up

PLANNING FOR A NO-DEAL

Angler
on a bulked pier.
He wears waterproof shorts.
Out with the bloody immigrants,
the lot

ELVIN THE BUILDER

From scratch
he's built his boat
moored at the River Stour
there he sleeps alone when he's drunk
too much

of London

THE CULT OF NATURE

He chats
with goldfinches,
blackbirds, house sparrows, tits
Sometimes they even answer him
backwards

BEFORE LONDINIUM

There was
a well so deep
where all the coins were thrown
a stone block where they gathered, cut
some throats

THE LOST PLANTS OF LONDON

Hare's-ear
London Rocket
Deptford Pink, Rough Clover
Green Hound's-tongue,
Hyssop Loosestrife Medlar

on Classics

AFTER PRUDENTIUS

Sleep tight
for night is all
there is: the limbs of men
their pain and grief. I too succumb
to this

RICHBOROUGH ROMAN FORT IN WINTER SOLSTICE

We perched,
looked west. Sunset
beyond the well kept fields
Portus Ritupis – elephant
asleep

AFTER READING BOETHIUS

On Earth
not much to see:
a road, few pilgrims, wars...
Books rare, but then people could read
the stars

A PRESENT

You brought
a well wrapped up
pink Cretan figurine
from 5BC. It glares at me
right now

ALCAEUS THE POET, HIS CUP

Let's drink
to the Muses
the long days, the short nights
Apollo's returned to Delphi,
so Cheers!

of the South of France

SUMMER AT VILLA LA VIGIE, 1924

Still life:
a mandolin
sleeps his sleep, a guitar
for a fandango. He dreamt of girls
and bull

PORTRAIT OF OLGA PICASSO (1920)

Her hand
on her draped lap
The head of a goddess.
She looks away, her sad eyes of
Lead White

KATHERINE MANSFIELD AT ISOLA BELLA

What views! –
she often said,
what air by the palm trees!
She coughed blood, her strength dimmed. Her life
cut short

AT PIERRE BONNARD'S MUSEUM

We saw
'Nude In The Bath'
You showed me the purple
glow, the stark amber tones. She, bathed
in light

MENTON

You asked
Would you live here?
I said yes, then thought, mmmh
But what about our house in Deal?
Erm... well...

How Do You Like them apples?[1]

J. KATES

WHENEVER I make a presentation about my work translating Russian-language poets, I have to begin with a disclaimer – I am neither a scholar nor a Slavist. I am a poet translating poems – the particular language the original poems are written in is almost secondary to this fact. When it comes to linguistic command, my Russian is inadequate and self-taught, although I confess a presumptuous affinity with the culture that enables me, in Mikhail Aizenberg's generous words, to make 'the right mistakes'.

For the most part, also, the Russian poets I have translated – however different in style and school – have been of my own generation and share many of my persuasions. My working relationships with them have been various, from collegial to *laissez-faire* to intrusive, but pretty much rely in the end on my own rooted American understandings in grounding the translations.

But, diffident as I am with regard to the Russian language, how much more distant from me is Central Asia? Russian serves as a shaky bridge I cross with trepidation. But for the Kazakhstani poet Aigerim Tazhi, born in 1981 in Aktobe – formerly Aktyubinsk – Russian is solid ground underfoot. 'I live in Kazakhstan', she has said, 'but I was born in the Soviet Union. . . . I did not choose the Russian language, did not evaluate it . . . It's just the language that I've spoken since childhood.'[2]

Fortunately for me, Tazhi also has a feel for English. Our collaboration (to extend the bridge) spans chasms of age and gender as well as culture, and somehow has proved remarkably productive and congenial for more than seven years now. Here are some elements we have discovered we share:

– a preference for letting the poem speak, and not the poet. We both recoil from injecting ourselves into the text, and from setting a poem in an autobiographical framework. This is why I publish using only my initial, and why Tazhi minimizes any personal information in contributor's notes and other writings around her work.

– going along with this, our poems themselves, different as they are in our separate styles, are concerned far less with ourselves than with the world around us. We both like to write from the inside out, rather than from the outside in. As I put it in my introduction to our book, Tazhi 'makes her own persona not the centre of attention, but the centre of perception'. I'd like to think that that's how someone might describe my poems, too.

– a predilection for form without being formalist – internal

rhymes and word-play come naturally to both of us, and we are both opportunistic rather than dogmatic. Sound and music matter as much as verbal accuracy. But also:
– an editor's tolerance for, even enjoyment in, wrestling precisely the exact image, the right word, not just the overall effect. This editorial delight does not always result in literal word-for-word correspondence in the translation, but rather governs a process that can pass between us in draft after draft, trying to get 'it', whatever 'it' might be, right.

A lot of this is intuitive on my part, not reasoned. A recent reviewer lauded my rendering of 'фонарик' in a line as 'flashlight' rather than as 'headlamp', and found good reason for the choice. I confess that neither I nor Tazhi had thought that out ahead of time – the vocabulary just seemed appropriate, and, when I had written that word in its place, neither of us questioned it. When she does challenge my word-choice, her offerings are often inspired beyond my imagining.

Other questions raised by the text between us are more cultural than linguistic, and here my own ignorance of the Kazakhstani landscape precedes the difficulty of communicating Tazhi's imagery to an equally ignorant American readership. 'Чесночные маковки' are what we could describe simply as 'onion domes' in English, but without (if I may say so) the pungency of the original double imagery of garlic and poppies. Still, these I can recognize on my own. What exactly is a шатёр in Tazhi's landscape? Certainly not in American usage a 'marquee', as she suggested to me from her dictionary, and something other than a 'tent' in its general sense, but dangerously not a 'big tent', with all those Western connotations. We feel our way around. For the purpose of the image, I eventually went with 'awning'. But I feel the inadequacy of this, even as I write it.

There is a theoretical translators' argument for immersing the English in the original, the original in the English. Somewhere (I can't remember where) G.K. Chesterton wrote that he had no idea what a *verst* is, but every time he reads the word, he knows he is in Russia. *Verst* works in English with only the vaguest of cross-cultural definition. I am reminded of this when Tazhi pleads with me in another exchange: 'Can't we just keep the word *aul*? After all, it's a specifically regional word, like, for example, *yurt*.' But *yurt*, I have to explain, is easily recognizable to a Western audience, and calls up immediately the accurate image of a Central Asian steppe, while *aul*, however familiar to Russian speakers, has to be looked up in a specialized dictionary. I had to look it up myself. It is several versts too far from our own landscape. I don't want to keep it in a literary translation for general readers.

In at least one labyrinthine case, Tazhi has appealed to my own understanding of Russian culture to catch a description and an image completely alien to the American consciousness: 'This is as in Petersburg, where one courtyard opens onto another through passages among the buildings, and they all twist in a labyrinth of courtyards and tunnels, and all the courtyards are like stone wells.' All this to get across three words in her original text. I know her reference very well, the difficulty is in conveying it – translating it – to those who know only New World architecture.

There may be an irony that Russian cultural references, like the Russian language, are the points of intersection of our work together. That's for others to tease out. I return to my starting point – almost total ignorance of Tazhi's Kazakhstani milieu. Would my translating be made easier if I could visit Almaty? Does reading help? Alas, there is little enough to read – I reiterate that I am not a scholar of the place and time, and I have found myself resorting to the pages of journals like the 2015 *Новый мир* devoted to Kazakhstani writers of Tazhi's generation.

Along the way, Tazhi has educated me. I thought I knew my apples, but the apples that roll through the poet's lines may be quite different from those I've ever seen or tasted: 'Really, we live on the other side of the moon. Alma-Ata has long been officially called Almaty now, and it is no longer the "the father of apples", alas – not by name, not in reality. I remember when I was a child Papa traditionally brought back from his trips to Almaty a single apple. An aport. That was the kind of apple it was, huge, like a canteloupe or a good-size teapot. We invited relatives in and ate it all together. That's what apples were like. But now the apples have grown smaller. After the collapse of the Soviet Union no one cared about orchards, they cut them down, they built mansions on the land.'[3]

This is the fertile fruitland of Aigerim Tazhi's poetry, which I import into the supermarket of Granny Smith and Red Delicious.

NOTES

1 This article is adapted from a talk given at the annual conference of the Association for Slavic, East European and Eurasian Studies in November 2019.
2 Interview with Philip Metres, translaed by Philip Metres, https://www.dispatchespoetrywars.com/commentary/sometimes-one-drop-enough-change-whole-ocean-aigerim-tazhi-interview-philip-metres-2014/
3 Слышится отдаленный звук, точно с неба, звук лопнувшей струны . . . .

(untitled)

I have a bitter heart
a tight ribcage
I walk the road out of town
into neighborhoods sprinkled on the hills
inhale a little air
and exhale a dance of words
others take the sky
for a ragged felt awning
winds futile gusts
by touch defective eyes
heart wrapped in wormwood
wounded behind its shutters
a stifling illusion of eyelids
destroyed by prisoners

(untitled)

twigs crackling in the fireplace
the snap of branches in a fog
I know what this is –
autumn
leaves cover my house up to the roof –
but we ask
who's there?
a knock at the door?
terrifying...
I see through the keyhole –
a faceless visitor...

(untitled)

godbearing cloud
gold-dappled apples
scattered outside the window

skin blanketed in buds
braids woven into cocoons
butterflies rhythmically rocked
on a rheumy wind

(untitled)

And you were there and the floor seemed to float
A blanket walked on naked feet
A creature nestled inside it

Hello, you're up? Breakfast on the table
Egg-yolk eyes skewed against the fork
Have frozen forever. So it will be.

Look at the deceptive way things go on
The tea cooled down, then rose again

From extinction with a single step
Prophetic, a glass ball glowed
Light broke down into pure shades

An onion bulb sprouted in a jar
Nothing under its husk. But a forest above.

And there your you disappeared, I disappeared

... It sniffed settled on a knee
Hot breath tucked into a neck

(untitled)

The wind meanders,
tousles hair
flies into a mouth
as a voice.
I whisper something
to dried leaves
treating the heart.
They listen.
A weeping wind
fills my matted,
crumpled sail
without knocking.
White hair
from the crown falls
the burden of overripe
years.

(untitled)

A word dropped from my lips.
(as if once again
I lived that shameful moment).

My heart burned,
I went cold.
You turned and walked away.
Laughing at our absurd meeting,
a bird dropped off
a shoulder turned to stone.

I, with a heart held fast in ice,
kept repeating
the words of the sentence.

(untitled)

I run after the sun towards its setting
at some time or another I will likely tire
but call to a winged companion
and fly on the tail of the autumn flock
as far as the line of another horizon
and exhausted there being simply a gray bird
I will declare my wanderings futile
and promise to settle down

(untitled)

A tree, like a windmill
is waving its arms at us.
In the fine flour your face,
the moon.
Frosted, chalk-white.
Bodies not visible at night.

Secretly sow with grass
a defunct dooryard
near the house. Arrows slid
to the edge. Time to go back.
The night smells of earth.
Seeds whisper.

Poems by Rocco Scotellaro

TRANSLATED BY CAROLINE MALDONADO

Rocco Scotellaro (1923–53) was born in Tricarico, a small town in Basilicata (previously known as Lucania) in the poor south of Italy, an area brought to the attention of the world by Carlo Levi in his book, Christ stopped at Eboli, written from his own experience of political exile and describing the deplorable conditions in the region. Lucania was then comparable to much of the developing world today: pollution and malaria were rife, peasants struggled to make a living. Scotellaro's lyrical and compassionate poems express his love for his land and its people, his anger and sorrow at their exploitation and at the destruction of their cultural identity and history. For a while Scotellaro left the South, first to study in Rome and then in search of work and to widen his experience of the world. He engaged with the contemporary literary scene, major writers such as Calvino, Montale and Pavese, and encountered the work of foreign writers, all of which contributed to his own development as a poet. Despite starting to find literary success, he chose to return to Lucania and at the still young age of twenty-three became a Socialist mayor of Tricarico, where he established a much-needed hospital. He died of a stroke at the age of thirty. His dear friend Levi edited a first collection of his poems posthumously and it was awarded the Pellegrino and Viareggio prizes in 1954. More of his poems can be found in Rocco Scotellaro, Your call keeps us awake, co-translated by myself with Allen Prowle, (Smokestack Books 2013).

Prisoner

The swishing of birds through air
suddenly wakes me.
Night's book has clapped shut
over my face.
I don't know
where I've been.
The hour founders
in dark time,
it hasn't called me.
Prisoner,
here's your key,
free, with no revenge, alive
but like a plant
closing its leaves
at evening.

In your mouth you'll have the taste of oranges

As our town rises at sunset
and Mount Vulture and the distant sun fall,
the express train, in a game of see-saw,
will have left you facing Naples,
that great beaker of shining glass.

Waves from the sea will reach your carriage,
in your mouth you'll have the taste of oranges:
the gesture you'll make
carries my heart to Naples.
I remember the first greeting of love,
your hand at the train window
is the most passionate kiss you've given me.

Bricklayers on their break

They line up by the railings in the square
where clusters of lights were lifted high
for the long-past feast day of the patron saint.
Their clothes and hands are white with lime,
they have dust in their eyes.
The song on the disc calling them
to their places in the cafe doesn't touch them.
They wait for the black clock to strike soon
and then they will climb back
onto the roofed terraces:
cats enter from the balconies
to lick the plates on laden tables.

Behind the Basento

It is the night's cold that stings me
and the corn husks
that screech at me under
the rusty ridge.
But over there behind the farm
beyond the pontoon bridge
near the pine grove
it is the howling of the fierce wolf,
the savage cry of the ewe lambs
running beyond the placid Basento.
The wind buzzing all round me
scares me: I lie stretched out.
Later, in the shadow of the full moon
it's the dog, it's the shepherd
who struggles with the wild beast
then flees for his life
over there in the wood where the wolf risks
ambush and where it stays, throat
slashed.
It is the wind that sends me to sleep
now that fear is dead inside the pen.

Three Poems

KATERINA ANGHELAKI-ROOKE

Translated from the Greek by Karen Van Dyck

When Katerina Anghelaki-Rooke was one year old, the celebrated writer and critic Nikos Kazantzakis stood as godfather at her baptism. When she was seventeen, he published her poem 'All Alone' in an Athenian magazine with a note saying that it was the most beautiful poem he had ever read. By her early twenties she was already an established poet. During the dictatorship (1967–74), she and a group of younger poets spearheaded a new kind of poetry that grappled with the confusion and censorship of those years. Meeting regularly with the translator Kimon Friar, they produced an anthology of six young poets, one of the first books to break the self-imposed silence initiated by the Nobel laureate poet George Seferis in response to the colonels' press laws. Linking the women poets of the previous postwar generation (Eleni Vakalo, Kiki Dimoula) to those of the generation of the 1970s (Maria Laina, Jenny Mastoraki), Anghelaki-Rooke stands out for the lyrical accessibility of her work. Hers is a poetry of flesh, indiscretion, and the divine all rolled into one. For Anghelaki-Rooke the body is a passageway anchoring the abstract metaphysics of myth in the rituals of everyday life. It is through the body that everything makes sense. As she once said: 'I do not distinguish the soul from the body and from all the mystery of existence... Everything I transform into poetry must first come through the body. My question is always how will the body react? To the weather, to aging, to sickness, to a storm, to love? The highest ideas, the loftiest concepts, depend on the morning cough...' In commemoration of her passing this year, here are three poems of eerie clarity from her last collection in which it is already clear she is looking at the world 'with other eyes' (2018). For other poems see the collection I edited: The Scattered Papers of Penelope: New and Selected Poems by Katerina Anghelaki-Rooke *(Anvil 2008).*

Epilogue Wind

Each time an act ends
humans feel the need
to write an epilogue
on paper or in the heart.
What was created by the mind
like lightning wants to shine
in the heaven of creation, to last
even if only in one small corner of history.
I find myself at that time of life
where I should 'epilogue'
but I feel my past disappear
leaving only faint tastes and images
with no explanation.
The wind is there, though,
sometimes wild, sometimes cool,
carrying with it storms or calm.
Yes, the wind is the right epilogue
to a complete life
which, of course, when asked why
has no answer.

With Other Eyes

The time came to see my life
with other eyes like a memory
left behind while searching for eternal emptiness,
frantic not to miss a sign I might interpret
from my dreams. Now I see reality
naked, without imaginary or real faces,
without love, life's spring, youth,
without the enthusiasm for every little creative act.
If I take down all the decorations
from the old reality
will I get clóser to the truth?
But how to conceive of truth
if it isn't full of living air?
No answer there. I sink into the night
and try again.

Memory, the Broken Toy

My memory was never very good
but I liked to play around
like when I'd ask: 'His eyes,
his arms, what were they really like?
Which day was the first day he had me?'
And if it was sunny inside
my imagination would come and fill in all the details.
But if sadness filled my soul
memory also went into mourning.
And now with my memory almost entirely gone
like a person no longer in my life
nothing from the past
lights up or clouds over.
But Oh! That smile!
The present, the absolute ruler
now. Pleased.

Mirrors and music

Pere Gimferrer's Catalan poetry in translation

TREVOR BARNETT

OVER THE LAST TWENTY YEARS, readers and critics in the English-speaking world have started to catch up with the idea that Spain's poetry is not always Spanish poetry. A significant proportion of the poetic output in Spain is not in the language of Cervantes, which is hardly surprising in a country where forty per cent of the population live in bilingual regions. In recent years, there have been several important translations into English of poetry written in three of Spain's regional languages: Galician, Basque, and Catalan. Whilst it is important to resist the nationalism and romanticism that sometimes underlies such endeavours, these translations have helped to change perceptions of poetry from Spain, particularly with English editions of the great Catalan writers. Now in *The Catalan Poems* we have the long-awaited first translation of Spain's greatest living poet, Pere Gimferrer.

Pere Gimferrer is a prolific poet, writer, critic, and translator, and he has long been recognised in Spain as one of the foremost intellectuals and original writers working today. Following his early success in Spanish – his second collection, *Arde el Mar* won Spain's National Poetry Prize in 1966 – Gimferrer emerged as one of the stars of a generation of poets called the *novísimos* (the newest ones), the name given to a group of poets who turned their backs on the social poetry of the previous decades. The generation were named after Castellet's seminal anthology, *Nueve Novísimos* (Nine Newest Ones), published in 1970. In that same year, Gimferrer's first collection of poems in Catalan was also published. Since then, as well as writing occasional works in French and Italian, Gimferrer has continued to alternate between writing poems in Spanish and in Catalan.

Until recently, Gimferrer had been overlooked in America and in the UK, but then three years ago Verba Mundi published a translation of his only novel, *Fortuny* (reviewed in PN Review 231), and now Carcanet have published a translation of his poetry in *The Catalan Poems.* This selection of poems will challenge those anglophone readers who believe that Spain's great poetry is limited to the Generation of '27 and to the Golden Age. Indeed, this book should prompt a critical re-evaluation, in the English-speaking world at least, of the possibilities of poetry in Spain. After all, Gimferrer's poetry is unlike that of any other Spanish poet because of its experimentation and its polyglossy. To understand a poet like Gimferrer requires an awareness not only of the unique traditions of Catalan poetry and Spanish poetry but also of the fluidity between them in his work. However, his poetry does much more than multilingual cross-pollination. Gimferrer's body of poems is like the architecture of Els Quatre Gats, the famous café in Barcelona: it is a beautiful composite structure of different styles and influences, from Medieval to Modernist. For over fifty years, Gimferrer has sought to revitalise poetry and push the limits of form. The publication of his poems in English will show the poetic landscape of modern Spain in a vivid new light.

The Catalan Poems focuses on Gimferrer's early works in Catalan – most of the translations are from books published in the 1970s and '80s – although nearly all of his Catalan poetry collections are represented. There are gaps though, for example, there is nothing here from his long poem *Mascarada* (Masquerade). Nevertheless, this selection displays Gimferrer's virtuosity and amplitude, and room has been given to some of the long poems, such as *L'espai desert* (Deserted Space), although shorter poems have inevitably been favoured.

The Catalan Poems is presented chronologically, so the reader can appreciate the development of Gimferrer's poetics over five decades. The book begins with five poems from *Els miralls*, his debut Catalan collection. The first poem from *Els miralls*, Snares, opens *The Catalan Poems*, and like a lot of his early poems, it shares many features with Gimferrer's Spanish poetry and with the work of the *novísimos*, such as the use of juxtaposition and pastiche. Allusion and intertextuality – prominent features throughout Gimferrer's work – also help to shape the poem. In only ten lines he has already referenced Wallace Stevens, Apollinaire, Juan Gris, Hölderlin, Goethe and Schiller. This is a poetry of signs and of signposts. Meaning is deferred, always elsewhere. The poem ends with a metatextual warning:

This poem is
a succession of snares:
for reader and
proofreader
and for the editor of the poem.

In *Els miralls* the poet is reflecting aspects of his Spanish poetic voice onto his nascent Catalan poetics, although this mirroring did not stop here: a few years later Gimferrer translated the collection into Spanish. In *Els miralls* the poet also begins to formulate an ars poetica. In Systems he writes:

Poetry is
a system of rotating,
mirrors, gliding harmoniously,
displacing light and shadow in the dressing room: why

the ground glass?

The mirror is a common metaphor for art, but Gimferrer pluralises the image as 'mirrors' to signal the multiplicity of meanings that the reader can find reflected in his work. His hermeneutic poems hold our gaze by reflecting not so much the world as the word.

Gimferrer produced several poetry collections in quick succession in the early 1970s in which he continued to experiment with lyric poetry in Catalan. While he began to establish differences in the poetics and the aesthetics of his Spanish poetry and his Catalan poetry, there remained considerable overlap between the two, as evident in the selections from *Hora foscant* (The Darkening Hour) and *Foc cec* (Blind Fire), for example, in the poems Vlad Drakul and Foc Cec. Gimferrer's *Tres poemes* (Three Poems), though, is unlike any of his Spanish poems from the period. He creates a new voice charged with metaphysical eroticism, as shown in the following extract from 'Visions':

> The red
> sky mimics the red waters of sunset:
> your body mimics nothing. Silence, bronze,
> suspended explosion, incandescences,
> nudity denying the night, blackening snow,
> hostage to this bedroom.

This metaphysical and sensory language is continued in his next collection, the ambitious long poem *L'espai desert* (Deserted Space), but now it is mixed within a secular mysticism, a fragmented, elliptical dream-vision. Gimferrer's style remains allusive and full of literary references, but the poem's form is influenced by the technique of collage as used by Max Ernst – Gimferrer, also a renowned art-critic, was writing a book about Ernst at the time he was composing *L'espai desert*. This collection shows Gimferrer's ongoing experimentation with enjambment and line length, as can be seen in this sample from the final section of the poem:

> Listening to the nothingness, inhaling an absence
> of air in a caisson, in a barometric
> zero, the hibernal void,
> in non-time and non-space, the void
> that tears at my lungs when I breathe
> until I feel breathed in by the void,
> the non-space that respires me, the formidable
> lungs, and I am the breathing,
> the breath of non-space, when it inhales
> and exhales...

Echoes of Eliot, Pound, and Gimferrer's favourite American poet, Wallace Stevens, are noticeable in these lines, as is the influence of Heidegger.

In *Apariciones* (Apparitions) Gimferrer again favours longer poetic forms, but at times he strips down his poetry to a lightly-spun pastoral:

> Queen of the canticle intoned by the willows
> queen of the seed that empties light,
> of the olive and the voices of grape clusters,
> queen of the brilliance of the belfry...

This is a mode of writing that has always been present in his Catalan works, but here it is quietly brought to the surface. The core of the poem, though, remains elusive. Reading Gimferrer is like looking through a reflection. Often, the poem's music is its meaning, as in the work of Wallace Stevens. In fact, Gimferrer's description of Steven's poetry later on in *The Catalan Poems* could easily be applied to his own work: 'Inevitably, it all flows together: the poem is the spectacle – mental and sensuous – of the process of poetry's creation.'

The title of Gimferrer's next collection, *Com un epíleg* (As an Epilogue), signals an end to this first cycle of creativity in Catalan. In *Com un epíleg* the poems are mostly brief meditations and epigrams on the natural world and on poetry, as can be seen in Poetic Art:

> More than bestowal of synthesis:
> to see in the light the transit of the light.

These poems also indicate the direction his future poetry would take; Gimferrer begins to move away from free verse to experiment with rhyme and sonnets. This transition towards more traditional poetic forms continues in *La llum* (Light) with an extraordinary sonnet sequence. The poet is now bolder in bending form to his own purposes. A poetry such as Gimferrer's presents many challenges to any translator, yet the translator, Adrian Nathan West, has succeeded in conveying Gimferrer's intertextual threads, its lexical vitality, and its euphony, as in the sestet of Apotheosis:

> The flambant tunics of windblown gods
> in a whisper of blood and gold on the rugs,
> the prayer of the air for volatile gods:
> a gong sounding out in the dolomite nights,
> the sword thrust of light of stalactites
> and a tumult of Sinbads in Turkesque robes.

At times Gimferrer seems to luxuriate in language, but his decision to opt for obscure and literary words is an important part of his aesthetic: he wants us to notice the beauty in each word and the music in each syllable. The translator pays close attention to these lexical textures and he uses loan words, calques and neologisms to recreate the experience of defamiliarization and to foreground the music.

The final poem in *The Catalan Poems* is taken from Gimferrer's penultimate collection, *El castell de la puresa* (The Castle of Purity), which was published in 2014. In this collection, as shown in this wonderful lyrical poem, Lay, Gimferrer is in dialogue not only with the poets who have accompanied him for years – Ausias March and J. V. Foix to name two – but also with his own early poetry, particularly his work in Catalan. The poem's allusions (the title of the collection comes from Stéphane Mallarmé via Octavio Paz), its hypnotic anaphora, and its lilting rhythms synthesise the qualities that make his best poetry so captivating and so beautiful. Here is a sample:

> if we are nothing but the thumb of the snow,
> aimed at the rock of parched light,
> light-parched, snow-parched, and there in the word
> we know to speak splendor ablaze in its cages,

like the moribund nightingale telling
when the mares of the darkness will approach.

In these lines, as on many occasions in *The Catalan Poems*, the translator has managed to convey, particularly through assonance and alliteration, much of the beauty and the music of the original.

The Catalan Poems also contains forty pages of his *Dietari*, an artistic diary in which the poet reflects on writers and artists, but especially on those poets who have directly influenced his own work, including Ezra Pound, Fernando Pessoa, Lucretius, Góngora, and Wallace Stevens. The writing here is highly original and incisive, for example, in 'The Secrets of Plagiarism'. The diary complements the poems not only because each entry is an indirect reflection on his own art and craft but also because the diary is one of the many manifestations of Gimferrer's lifelong experimentation with genre and form. In fact, the diary entries can be read as extensions of the poems; they share the same music and deliver similar doses of metatextuality and allusion as in Twilight when he writes 'In 1891, Claude Monet, painter, looked, from one day to the next, at this strange fluvial artefact, the fugitive splendor of the poplars during the final fifteen minutes of twilight'. For Gimferrer, forms and genres are fluid and they spill into each other – a diary can become biography, a prose poem can become literary criticism, a novel can become something so unlike a novel that it defies all generic labels. The book closes with a recent interview with the poet which provides further critical insight into his work. In the interview transcript the reader will recognise just how much of Gimferrer's poetic voice – his erudition, his digressions, his wit – mirrors his conversation and vice versa.

In his prologue to the Spanish version of *El castell de la puresa* Gimferrer describes poetic language in Catalan today as 'a vast, beating body', yet this organic metaphor could just as easily be applied to his own coherent, fascinating oeuvre. *The Catalan Poems* brings this body of poems to life for readers in English. The book shows Gimferrer's experimentation with form, his richly allusive music, and the interplay between his writing in Spanish and in Catalan. All this makes it essential reading not only for anyone interested in poetry from Spain but for anyone who is drawn to poetry that challenges as much as it delights.

From the Archive

Issue 153, September–October 2003

MONIZA ALVI

From 'Three Poems after Jules Supervielle'. Fellow contributors to this issue include Gerard Woodward, Kate Clanchy, Richard Bush, John Peck and Michael Palmer.

from THREE POEMS
AFTER JULES SUPERVIELLE

Riderless Horses

Once there was a cavalry troop,
long dispersed.
The horses would soak their necks in the future
so they could gallop on and on.

They were wild and tireless.

Sleek black, fearful,
they'd run in all directions,
spin round in circles,
stopping only to die,
change pace in the dust, and start again.

The frantic colts would catch up with the mares.

So many horses have passed this way
and nothing is left of them
but the beating of their hooves.

Let me listen to the hoof beats of my past –
my former heart beating in its glade.

And let the heart I'm stuck with now
give way, drunk - with the brevity of life.

Tell Our Story

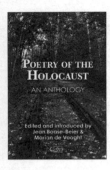

Poetry of the Holocaust: An Anthology, edited and introduced by Jean Boase-Beier and Marian de Vooght (Arc Publications) £12.99

Reviewed by TARA BERGIN

John Felstiner was speaking as a practitioner when he said that 'translation is the art of loss'. For readers, translation is always the art of gain. Even the losses are gains; and sometimes, as in the case of Holocaust poetry, the losses can feel anachronistically integral to the whole process of transference.

This is not about the aesthetic appeal of rough literals or the conscious use of impoverished English in the final versions. Rather, it's about the way that an increased awareness of the translator's task can re-focus our attention on the words a poet uses to make a poem. When translation is placed in the foreground, we are encouraged to think further about what we are reading, and where it came from. As with Michael Schmidt's recent study of 'Gilgamesh' (Princeton, 2019), when the re-telling becomes part of the life of the poem, its existence becomes 'on-going'.

It's partly this focus on translation that makes Arc's new anthology, *Poetry of the Holocaust*, so interesting and unusual. With thirty-five translators working from nineteen languages, including Norwegian and Japanese, the collection places specific emphasis on giving a voice to those less frequently heard from in books of Holocaust poetry: the Roma, the Sinti, the gay, the disabled, the mentally ill. Some of these poems have never appeared in English before now, and the editors' provision of brief biographies before every poem means we learn the fate of every poet before we read what they have written: imprisoned, hanged, beheaded, killed by dogs, gassed. We hear from Judith Kerr's father (who survived), and Paul Celan's niece (who didn't). We learn about the blue buses in Riga, used to round up Jews and other unwanted people; we learn about the stinking 'Dysentery Barracks' and the hospital where thousands were killed because they were mentally ill. We learn about the poets' own 'skinny legs' and 'naked hands', and about one Unknown Youth who gives his age as 'nineteen plus two' – he's twenty-one, but he can't bear to count the years he spent in Plötzensee Prison.

'The individual voice is everything', write the editors in the introduction, and this is a crucial point. Above all else, this is a book of voices; a collection not just of poems but also of testimonies: statements, declarations, evidence. Furthermore, so the editors suggest, when we know we are receiving these poems in translation, the act of communication is even more poignant. If poetry is resistance, they write, 'translated poetry is a double act of resistance'.

How to decide what poems should appear in an anthology such as this? The focus on translation was clearly an important factor. There are no poems by any English-language Holocaust poets here: their work, argue the editors, is already widely accessible to English speakers. They also omit any readily available translations. This means that the most famous Holocaust poem of all, Paul Celan's 'Death Fugue', has been left out. Yevtushenko's 'Babi Yar' is excluded for the same reason, while Hungarian poet János Pilinszky is omitted for a different one. The editors explain why in their fascinating introduction, and while these gaps are at first disappointing, they do serve to drive home the purpose of this book, which is not to replace but to add. Read as an extension to our existing anthologies, this book proves essential. See for example Charlotte Serre's short poem, 'The Camp', written in Ravensbrück, and quoted here in its entirety:

> Horror, terror, hunger, blows,
> Flames, the walls, the whip, the cold,
> Lice and roll-call, dogs and snow...
>
> The watch-tower...
>
> Turn... turn... carousel...

Poetically, Ted Hughes's English version of Pilinszky's 'The Passion of Ravensbrück' has more formal finality, but Serre's first-hand account, translated from the French by Timothy Adès, sheds new light on Hughes's powerful depiction of a shaven-headed male prisoner.

Poetry of the Holocaust: An Anthology arose out of a research project entitled 'Translating the Poetry of the Holocaust', carried out at UEA in 2013–14. Around that time, I attended a talk about the project, in which Jean Boase-Beier discussed her translation of Celan's poem, '*Totenhemd*' (literally 'death-shirt', but translated by Boase-Beier as 'Winding Sheet'). Celan survived the Holocaust but his parents were killed, and he committed suicide in 1970 by drowning in the Seine. In her talk, Jean Boase-Beier mentioned that Celan's mother used to knit him jumpers, and that he wore them long after she was killed. For years after that I imagined the jumpers were black, until I read in John Felstiner's biography that Celan's mother had knitted coloured sweaters for him, which made the image even sadder. But then, everything seems sadder when you learn more about the Holocaust. This anthology makes for harrowing reading, but it is also historically and linguistically and poetically necessary. As the introduction makes clear, 'the time after the Holocaust is still ongoing'. We must keep the stories alive.

Illicit Trakl

Georg Trakl, *Surrender to Night: Collected* Poems, selected and translated by Will Stone (Pushkin Press) £15

Reviewed by BRIAN MORTON

There is a minor slip in [translator] Will Stone's introduction that delivers a happy coinage. He says quite rightly that Trakl's poetry has been the object of unceasing debate for more than a century (there is a rival new translation abroad by James Reidel, from Seagull Books) but then adds that 'the resulting presentations may illicit [sic] admiration, from the reader, but also frustration'. It is not immediately clear whether this frustration comes from the poems or the interminable debate, but no matter: 'illicit admiration' is exactly what Trakl invites, together with an emotion other than frustration. If there is a such a thing as a guilty pleasure, then devouring page after page of verse that plays on a narrowed bandwidth of themes – evening, silence, animals, colour, death – without understanding much of what is going on must count as one. Even Wittgenstein, who admired Trakl and sent money to keep him solvent, admitted he didn't have a clue, and if for Wittgenstein, the limits of our words were the limits of our world, then Trakl inhabited a very small one at best. And yet we keep on reading him.

The effect, if we stick with guilty pleasures, is like eating a box of liqueur chocolates, one after the other. After a while, the flavours become undifferentiated and the intense sensation gives way to a queasy guilt. Trakl's addictions were more severe. Working in pharmacy kept him close to the drugs he depended on. Circumstance and marriage kept him away from Grete, the gifted sister he doted on and may, if the palpable wish were ever enacted, have known incestuously. His world, like his words, was tightly circumscribed and landlocked. Until the First World War offered him a second spell in uniform, his life was limited to Salzburg, Innsbruck and Vienna, which should explain the landlocked character of his themes.

There is no ozone in Trakl's poetry, nothing of the oceanic. As Stone repeats, because others have said it before him, Trakl ploughed a very narrow furrow, but ploughed it deep. Michael Hamburger, in his introduction to Carcanet's *Georg Trakl: A Profile* (published in 1984, when the Trakl-in-English business was just hotting up), said that of the three voices of poetry, the young Austrian only had the first: that is, the poet talking to himself, with no consciousness of an audience. That may be the impression, but it is an incomplete one. Trakl placed more than sixty of his poems in Ludwig von Ficker's *Der Brenner*. Because of his early death, we tend to read him as if the work were discovered posthumously, yellowing in a trunk, but not so. He liked solitude, but was showy with his work, and it reads that way. If it can be dismissed as a wholesale borrowing from Hölderlin, with a little Rimbaud thrown in, it soon turned into self-plagiarism, in which subject and style bordered on manner.

Stone captures the music of Trakl's verse well enough, but inconsistently, and this comes in part from his failure to see the work in anything other than autobiographical terms. What Reidel succeeds in doing is alerting us to the specificity and historicity of Trakl's language and themes, his intuitive commentary on a world that was tearing itself apart and reconstructing itself in what passes for real time in such circumstances. Psychoanalysis and eugenics were building themselves into the discourse of the day; militarism and socialism pulled in opposite directions; industrial technology had begun to supplant the hand-carved; and Trakl saw all this and responded to it. Probably no society before America in the 1950s was more profoundly medicated than Austria on the cusp of the First World War. Cocaine, with which Freud had experimented in 1884, three years before Trakl was born, was being stockpiled for the troops, and as Richard Millington has shown in *Snow From Broken Eyes*, exerted a powerful, albeit very different, influence on the work of Trakl, Gottfried Benn (who was also a physician) and Walter Rheiner. What a new translation needs to deliver is a poet who is both distant and very contemporary, someone genuinely transitional, if that word means anything.

Stone's translations somehow don't quite deliver that. Simple line-by-line comparison doesn't prove much, but the tonal differences and choices add up. To focus on the less-known, uncollected poems, Stone gives 'Chamber concerts on a spiral staircase die out' for '*Kammerkonzerte, die auf einer Wendeltreppe verklingen*', this from the second version of '*Am Rand eines alten Wassers*' (which shifted in title between 'old fountain' and 'old waters'). Reidel renders the same line as 'Chamber concertos that fade away up a winding staircase', which is truer to mood, rhythm and sense. Not to overdo such comparison, Stone gives 'Rock loneliness is all around' for '*Ringsum ist Felseneinsamkeit*'. In '*St-Peters-Freidhof*', where Reidel has 'On all sides a rock solitude', which better answers to the deep pulse of Trakl's original, and its place in the continuum of his works.

The truth is that these are poems that can *only* be gorged like chocolates, even if some of the fillings are not to taste. There is an underlying musicality to Trakl that is preserved in Frank Graziano's Carcanet collection [*Georg Trakl: A Profile*] and in Reidel's. This is why the work can be danced, as choreographer Lake Angela showed in 'Silence Spoken… quiet answers to dark questions' some years ago; it can be found on YouTube.

Trakl's fate awaited him on the Eastern Front, a theatre whose utter grimness has been largely hidden from us by the hegemony of Anglophone 'war poets'. Of the two incontestably great poems in Trakl's output, 'Helian' from the 1913 *Gedichte* and 'Grodek', named after the autumn 1914 battle of Gródek (Horodok, and now in Ukraine) and published in *Der Brenner*, the latter is perhaps the better known, because of its proximity to Trakl's suicide. It is not war poetry in the conventional sense, more an inkling of how war emerges in the male psyche. Dying warriors with shattered mouths are present, but so, too, is the adored sibling. Michael Hamburger rendered '*Es schwankt der Schwester Schatten durch den schweigenden Hain*' as 'The sister's shade now sways through the silent copse', while Stone prefers the less ambiguous 'shadow' and the more obviously poetic 'grove'. Both capture the sibilant, sub-erotic mystery of the line, as other translators have done before them.

Stone delivers the work in orderly form, including the 1913 *Poems,* the posthumous *Sebastian im Traum,* and the poems published in *Der Brenner,* plus sixty pages of uncollected verse and prose and a valuable time-line of Trakl's life; none of the letters, which were such a valuable and illuminating component of *Georg Trakl: A Profile.* The voice of the letters is the voice of the various dream-selves – Elis, Sebastian, Kasper Hauser – that populate the poems, the brilliant adolescent who could declare to Ludwig von Ficker that 'indescribably shattering events' have overtaken him and will either destroy or 'perfect' him; and by the way, here is a poem I would like you to publish, 'Untergang', newly revised: 'The first version contains something only hinted at.' This is Trakl at his most mysterious, most human and most male, the side that attracted Rilke, wallowing a little in the unsayable, but also addicted to the second thought; he was a passionate reviser. Alexander Stillmark's parallel edition remains the best option for serious study, Reidel's for the music, Robert Grenier's, Michael Hamburger's, David Luke's and Christopher Middleton's in the Carcanet edition for clarity; Stone's, in its stubby, hand-friendly format, is the one you'd most likely stick in a jacket pocket en route to Salzburg or Innsbruck.

The Art of Losing

Marvin Thompson, *Road Trip* (Peepal Tree) £9.99

Reviewed by JOE CARRICK-VARTY

'A question is an utterance which typically functions as a request for information, which is expected to be provided in the form of an answer' – Wikipedia. I've been thinking a lot about questions lately. In poetry and in real-life. This era of smart phones, mass media, instant information could spell, in more ways than one, the end of the question, or at least, the end of that novel sense of *not knowing*. 'What's the weather going to be like tomorrow?' 'What's the weather going to be like in Athens tomorrow?' 'What chance is there, exact to a percentile, of rain in Athens tomorrow?' These are all questions I could ask my phone right now. All questions I could, within a second (Wi-Fi permitting), get an answer to.

I have to say Marvin Thompson's *Road Trip* is a life-affirming lesson in lostness, in being lost, in losing people, hope, one's sense of self, one's sense of belonging to a world where 'a taxi driver / on a Kingston / roadside / branded me, / my parents, / my brothers / English. / Not Jamaican.' A world where '150,000 larches / have been / felled.' A world where 'starlings / rise and rise / into the dusk's reds'. Because it's the poet's ear for wonder that makes this book so special – the urge to search, to find, to question.

'A question is an utterance which typically functions as a request for information, which is expected to be provided in the form of an answer'. Let's break that down – 'expected to be provided in the form of an answer'. So, a question is a kind of contract, a deal, a bridge of sorts, between an utterer in ignorance and an utterer in-the-know. Great. My kind of deal this question business. To ask a question is to admit ignorance, is to not only become vulnerable, but to actively make oneself vulnerable.

Many times, while reading *Road Trip*, I shivered, spat tea out, left the house just to walk somewhere. Because when Marvin Thompson asks a question you feel it; know it has been asked:

'born in London, / was I English / like school's / *niggers out* / graffiti?'

'What if / Derys and Hayden / choose / to identify / as White / in a Britain / that will call them / Black?'

'Will my fury be passed onto my children?'

In 'The one in which', a powerful and startling sequence assembled around a trip to the cinema, a parent struggles to come to terms with the identity of their Mixed Race children. Like many of the poems in *Road Trip*, the act of driving takes on the act of asking a question, of searching out an answer, as the rainy streets of a Welsh town are infused with 'Joe Harriott's abstract jazz...art that sings / Africa's diaspora'. The tension is something to behold as 'Cymbals shimmer' and the speaker smiles: 'my Mixed Race children are listening / to something I want them to love'. But, as ever, lostness pervades: 'Is this upbringing / or brainwashing?'

Later in the sequence the speaker will admit: 'One day, I'll tell Derys that I hoped she'd have afro hair', before a final arrest, in question form again: 'Should I be happier / that she fits into her White Welsh world?'

Road Trip is a heartbreakingly important debut.

Line Drawing

Christopher Reid, *A Scattering* and *Anniversary* (Faber) £10.99

Reviewed by EDMUND PRESTWICH

Christopher Reid's *A Scattering*, first published in 2009, was a loving but unsentimental tribute to his wife, the actress Lucinda Gane who died in 2005. *Anniversary*, thirteen pages of poems written ten years later and combined with it here, fittingly completes the story, although none of the new poems seems to me as vividly animated or memorable as the best in *A Scattering*.

Reid's writing has a fast-talking, conversational spring and his phrasing leaps between poles of colloquialism, even slang, on the one hand, and literary sophistication on the other. This is ideal for projecting a lively engagement with life, and for capturing Gane's own quirky vitality. As we see in the poems describing a holiday in Crete after Gane's cancer diagnosis, it's also ideal for interlacing such engagement with stabs of recognition of what is to come. It's a style well fitted to open-eyed, unflinching living with the whole situation that Reid and Gane find themselves in, seizing the good without averting eyes from the bad.

Colloquial immediacy is complemented by an opposite aspect of Reid's work. In some ways it's very formal, playing long, complicated sentence constructions against elegantly balanced metrical patterns. This in itself suggests intellectual and emotional control. Formalising fear, loss, grief and love, it respects the public nature of a book, and the reader's position as an outsider to the poet's experience. *A Scattering* as a whole becomes a kind of ceremony, linked by the title poem to an apparent funeral rite of elephants whereby they scatter the bones of any elephant skeleton they come on. These are not poems that grab the reader by the lapels and howl their emotion into his face. Dignity and restraint are essential to their style, even when Reid presents himself as a comic figure or, in poems of the 'Widower's Dozen' section, describes how bereavement caused derangements of perception in the form of overwhelmingly intense, reason-defeating hallucinations of Gant's physical presence.

A reward of this restraint is the clean clarity and beauty of a poem like the first in the 'Unfinished' section. Here's its opening:

> Sparse breaths, then none –
> and it was done.
>
> Listening and hugging hard,
> between mouthings
> of sweet next-to-nothings
> into her ear –
> pillow-talk-cum-prayer –
> I never heard
> the precise cadence
> into silence
> that argued the end.
> Yet I knew it had happened.

It's like a delicate line drawing in the way it uses the simplest possible vocabulary and syntax to lay the moment bare, presenting facts unclouded by emotive rhetoric. Skilful punctuation by line ending slows it so that we focus on every detail and listen intently to the white space silence around the words. The essential emotions arise from the situation itself, rather than being pushed at us by the poet. At the same time, simplicity is interwoven with a more sophisticated register that keeps our minds moving, like the use of 'cadence' instead of 'fall', or the richly packed, wonderfully suggestive conflation of pillow talk and prayer. Separating the components of this defensively terse phrase brings home the gulf between the warm intimacy of pillow talk in a pre-cancerous *then* and the poet's hopeless prayer beside the death bed *now*. Everywhere, it seems to me, the quiet tone makes the words a finely transmissive medium for the poet's feelings, so that, for example, one understands the rightness of 'argued' as against 'showed' in the penultimate of those lines by seeing how it suggests the poet's momentary futile resistance to accepting that she really has gone now.

Palpable in Absence

Mimi Khalvati, *Afterwardness*
(Carcanet) £9.99

Reviewed by MAITREYABANDHU

In his *Paris Review* interview, Geoffrey Hill, responding to a question about the 'difficulty' of his poems, said 'Human beings are difficult. We're difficult to ourselves, we're difficult to each other...' This is true. But to think of those difficulties as somehow intellectual difficulties requiring 'difficult' poetry to express them is absurd. Mimi Khalvati feels no need to do that in her new collection. *Afterwardness* is a sequence of fifty-six Petrarchan sonnets that meditate on a central difficulty of life: a void 'palpable in absence'.

This absence probably came into her life at the age of six when Khalvati moved from her native Tehran to a boarding school on the Isle of Wight. In that move 'first languages, half-formed, [were] dropped at the border' ('Dreamers'). 'What if a heritage were lost en route?' she asks in 'Mehrabad Airport'. What if the past becomes 'a book with no plot, story, timeline, no protagonists even / and no witnesses to events' ('Life Writing')? The crucial achievement of this collection, Khalvati's most ambitious and personal so far, is to write an emotionally-convincing sonnet sequence that circumambulates a void; a book whose subject is absence.

Except 'absence' suggests loss and pain, the sense of having lost some cherished thing. But these poems are too rigorous for certainties. One of Wallace Stevens' 'Thinkers without final thoughts', Khalvati interrogates the vacuum at the centre of *Afterwardness* for meanings and feelings in a sonnet-essay on difficult truthfulness:

> Why did I say I minded things I didn't –
> soul-making things I'd find too crude to name?
> Or silently collude with heartfelt, well-meant
> sympathy it seemed churlish to disclaim?
>   ('Chamaeleonidae')

Here as elsewhere, Khalvati's voice is individual yet unassertive, neither claiming the reader's attention nor rebuffing it. Her subtlety of thought, emotional precision and lyric openness treat the reader as a grown-up person who can *read*, not a child gloating over a comic book of moral instruction or political virtue. Khalvati's undemonstrative confidence – *Afterwardness* is a masterclass in how to think poetically – make it easy to overlook just how good the poems are. Each line is perfectly weighed, neither thin nor over-stuffed. Free from political markers and right-on posturing, *Afterwardness* explores child immigration and the loss of culture and language without melodrama or self-pity. Elizabeth Bishop said 'Although I think I have a prize "unhappy childhood"... please don't think I dote on it'. Khalvati in the same vein won't dote on identity, preferring the truthfulness of not being sure:

> Although she barely knew at school, at seven,
> what a Moslem was or what Islam meant,
> she proudly wrote: 'I know I'm not a Christian',
> reassuring her mother, 'but for Lent
>
> I have given up saying Honestly.'
>   ('The Lesser Brethren')

If not knowing, not feeling, not being at home, not belonging are central to this collection (and they are), then the poems of *Afterwardness* are also gloriously open to sweet spots and love in 'This vague and dream like world' (quoting Virginia Woolf in 'September').

The best way to read (and re-read) this collection is in a single sitting, relishing the key changes whilst going with the flow: childhood – 'A line of c's is like a stylised sea' ('Handwriting') – meets old age; the Aziziyeh Mosque gazes down on the Kentish ragstone of a Baptist Church ('Facades'); a mother's lighter illuminates a son's dysphagia; swing skirts meet hairslides and *Swann's Way*. The single lyric arc of *Afterwardness* – which begins with a child sitting in a plane and ends with an adult watching a plane from below – contains multitudes. Thought sparks off thought, each vividly particular and yet part of the flow. And with consummate skill Khalvati finds in juxtapositions and uncertainties, disparate things, a deeper imaginative unity, a palpable presence and a just as palpable absence.

Though Khalvati won't sensationalise loss, there's no doubt that absence haunts *Afterwardness* (the word 'void', for instance, reoccurs across the collection). Absence of history, place, narrative, staging posts, and language are as vivid in their absence as the missing diamond on an old engagement ring. This missingness is felt in the sea 'always there at walking distance', as 'palpable in absence as in presence' ('Torbay'), in the arrangement of furniture 'in lines around the walls, leaving the floor/ alone as the focal point' ('The Introvert House'), in the word *parandeh* for bird 'long since flown out of the mind' ('Translation'), and finally in a jet's contrail stretching the 'aftermath / into a lyric void' ('Vapour Trails').

For its uncluttered voice, its depth of poetic thought and seemingly effortless, unobtrusive rhyme (every line of this collection rhymes); for its glimpse of streets and mothers, 'the loneliness of women's live' ('Smiles'), ayatollahs, and 'little bits of nothing', these sonnets – not one of them routine – are an ideal companion for those of us who feel both at home and estranged in this serious-tender, difficult world.

Harps and Horns

W.D. Jackson, *Opus 3* (Shoestring Press) £15

Reviewed by CHRIS MCCULLY

It must have represented a risk, to both publisher and writer, to produce a work of 483pp. (nearly 100 of them, notes) and one moreover containing some material which has appeared in book form before (e.g. Jackson's *Boccaccio in Florence* and *Afterwords*). Nor is it usual for any reviewer to be confronted with any poetic opus of such scale and ambition: Jackson's comment that his work 'is nothing if not eclectic' (p.389) is perfectly just. The notes here, as well as the poetic reworkings and translations, range from Biblical accounts of Abraham through Ovid, Villon, Dante, Boccaccio; medieval romances, Chaucer and Shakespeare; Milton and Wordsworth; through translations (very fine translations, so far as I can judge them) from Heine and Rilke; to adaptations of (perhaps better, conversations with) Eliot and Borges. Engaging with Jackson's work is in itself a literate education. It is also a philosophical one: there is a seriousness lying behind Jackson's engagement with the materials and models provided by the past – an imaginative past which is here only too wonderfully present – which pushes almost all his work in the direction of a further engagement with ethics. If one cannot (and one cannot) equate goodness with success – as was Auden's worry when he renounced 'Spain', whose concluding lines seemed to offer such an equation - what then, in the baleful sweep of human history, *is* good conduct? What can history and its writers say not only to its 'defeated' (thus Auden, in lines he famously and subsequently rejected) but to its exterminated?

By coincidence, I'm writing these words on the 75th anniversary of the liberation of Auschwitz. 'If way to the Better there be, it exacts a full look at the Worst,' as Hardy put it (*In Tenebris* II, used also as an epigraph to *Opus 3* No.2, p.127), and in one of the most impressive central sections of *Opus 3* – 'Case Studies, 1941-1945' – Jackson explores voices and themes from the death-camps. He is unsparing, including not only the voices of those who argued for less brutal policies (voices over-ruled: 'Word came:/ *Try quicker, cleaner methods. Dynamite. Gas*', p.180) but those of self-disgusted observers (pp.185-86), camp Kommandants (e.g. SS-Oberscharführer Kurt Franz, who would set his dog onto Jews who did not learn the work-song he had written for them) and the voice of Reinhard Heydrich, whose 'Mental Notes for Conference' are here set in tabulated form ('2.1 Estimated number of Jews (incl. England and Ireland) to be liquidated: 11 Million', p.181). As in the supremely unsettling *Conspiracy* (dir. Frank Pierson, 2001) one is obliged to imagine – to reconstruct – extermination by committee. Yet here, too, the architecture of Jackson's work in *Opus 3* insists that all readers are implicated: 'Case Studies' forms part of a larger section of text titled 'Self-Portrait as a White-Collar Worker' (p.137), whose opening includes surface translations of

Heine and others (thus *du bist wie eine blume* is rendered as 'do pissed v. iron a bloomer', p.153). These juxtapositions, taken together with the fact that the poetry here embodies what it describes, render all songs upset and all voices – even the most apparently, effortlessly reasonable – deranged. Even more impressively, Part I of *Opus 3, No.2* begins with a series of what are ostensibly self-portraits in verse: the writer, too – and all the local histories which generate the derangements to come - is implicated. The fact that Jackson achieves this while maintaining such precision and formal control left me both admiring and aghast. To those ethical questions the work surely generates Jackson is wise enough to supply no answers; instead, he supplies a magnificent, disconcerting orchestration of human voices.

I've touched on Jackson's formal control. He is a master of prosodic structure. Like some of his colleagues, Villon, Boccaccio and Chaucer, Jackson is able to align a highly-constrained line with the cadences of the spoken voice not only by using contemporary diction but also exploiting the thematic potential of enjambment (i.e. where the enjambed material at the beginning of a following line is thematised or foregrounded): 'Abandoned children cried. The sick were left/*To die alone*, their bodies left to rot...' (p.11, my emphasis).

'Boccaccio in Florence' (p.11ff.) is replete with such effects, as are the Shakespearean sonnets which occupy part of *Opus 3, No.3* (pp.304-324). Here, characters from the plays speak of, or for, their condition. Thus the Earl of Warwick (from *Henry VI*, 1-3):

> At Towton even I lost heart – until,
> Trampled by hooves, my dying brother cried
> To me to take revenge....

And the final couplet, with its apt pun: 'Measure for measure *must* be paid. If not, / Mere vice or folly reigns – all roses rot.' (P.311).

The final sonnet in the sequence is given to Shakespeare:

> *...Strange then – absurd –*
> *How seldom poets see or say things right.*
>
> *Mine are all fools. Or liars on the make.*
> *Kit Marlowe – Chaucer – all too few – perhaps*
> *Were not. We poets are only people. Take*
> *us all in all, dogs squabbling over scraps...*
> [italics in the original]

'Only people...' – yes, of course. But by that time within the imaginative world of *Opus 3*, poets-who-are-only-people align with the terrors, absurdities, negations, despairs and wry joys embodied in or occasioned by other's voices. There is no privilege; there is only and ever the difficult acuity of witness.

I was also delighted to encounter a version of *Sir Orfeo*, an earlier medieval romance I last studied as an undergraduate. (The original is found in the Auchinleck MS, dating from c.1330.) Its most-quoted (and disputed) lines refer to the fairy hunt, apparently a Celtic motif; this is heard distantly, at one point in the original, 'with dim [or *dun*] cri and bloweing'. Jackson renders this as:

> ..swarms of bright forms appeared and listened,
> leaving a trail of dust, which glistened
> briefly behind them when they fled.
> Orfeo followed as far as it led...
>
> That night he played again.
>   Between
> bushes and trees, a King and Queen
> rode out to hunt on unicorns
> like shifting shadows. Their huntsmen's horns
> silenced his harp....

Taken as a whole, *Opus 3* is important work. I have come across nothing like it. The engagement is amply rewarded: Jackson's metrical and lexical skill is often as entertaining as his themes are provocative and his thought profound. I'm sure that other reviewers will find, if they have not already found, that a periodical review offers scant ambit in which to describe or delineate the ambition or scope of *Opus 3* – this would need a thesis – nor to engage in any serious way with the important questions that ambition and scope generate: how, as writers, can we engage with the past if we wish to do so as more than pasticheurs? Does pastiche or collage simply relativise evil into non-existence? If we are all implicated, where does the guilt go? Where should it go? In reply, one could do worse than to re-read the final section of text from *Opus 3*, an epilogue from Rilke whose opening this is:

> *Rilke: "O, sage, Dichter, was du tust"*
>
> Say, poet, what it is you do? – *I praise.*
>
> But Death and nightmare mar our days:
> How can you stand, how stomach them? – *I praise...*

A Sustainable Ecstasy

Charles Wright, *Oblivion Banjo*
(Farrar, Straus & Giroux) £38.90

Reviewed by M.C. CASELEY

Despite a stint as US Poet Laureate and his 1997 collection *Black Zodiac* winning a Pulitzer Prize, Charles Wright retains a comparatively low profile in this country compared to, say, Denise Levertov or John Ashbery. This generous selection, spanning seventeen of his books from the period 1973 to 2014, is an ideal starting-point for anyone wishing to explore his distinctive voice.

My first encounter with it came when Stride published the 1998 *Zone Journals* in this country, roughly halfway through his career, and I then worked backwards to *Country Music*, a 1982 gathering of his early work. *Zone Journals* is fairly representative of mid-period Wright, pushing his long, imagistic, broken line as far as it will go, free verse wearing a mask similar to narrative, colloquial prose. The early work in *Country Music*, on the other hand, the constituent parts of which occupy the first hundred pages here, reveals a more orthodox voice, one heavily indebted to Pound.

In many interviews, Wright has pinpointed one Pound poem, 'Blandula, Tenulla, Vagula', which he came across whilst living in Italy in 1959, working for the US Army. Travelling the Italian countryside, he encountered places mentioned by Pound and this was foundational to his early poetic awakening and development. It is fitting, therefore, that this volume begins with 'Homage to Ezra Pound', in which he salutes the 'cold-blooded father of light', a survivor in self-imposed silence. Wright's poems, too, are full of place-names, incantations of the American South, Virginia, Charlottesville, and his own landscapes. He has acknowledged himself as a Southern writer, interested in pushing the possibilities of the long line as far as it will go (including the possibilities of his characteristic step-down lineation). Although he does not profess to be a Christian, they also feature what he has called his arguments with God, stemming from his upbringing and education in the Episcopalian Church. In his poetry, landscape is always on the verge of the numinous, even as it surfaces in the quotidian and everyday.

It is difficult to excerpt from the long, submerged, epic scope of Wright's poems – perhaps another Poundian legacy – but here's a typical example:

> From my balcony, the intense blue of the under-heaven,
>   sapphiric and anodyne,
>   backdrops Madonna's crown,
>   later, an arched stretch of cloud,
>   like a jet trail or a comet's trail,
>   vaults over it,
> a medieval ring of Paradise.
> Today, it's that same blue again, blue of redemption...
>   ('A Journal of the Year of the Ox', *Zone Journals*)

The easy colloquial tone, the step-down lines, the transfigured landscape in the service of a concealed, impressionistic narrative – all these are staple features of Wright's poetics. The journalising of the *Zone Journals* pieces fed into later volumes like *Black Zodiac* and *Appalachia* as he continued to free up his poetic line, and their impact is best felt incrementally.

There are recognisable Wright landscapes, stances and modes of thinking and his later collections show how he continued to refine these, often making them more concise. *A Short History of the Shadow* (2002), for instance, includes many shorter poems which demonstrate how religion continues to bother him, now in an Appalachian setting:

> On Locust Avenue the fall's fire
> collapses across the lawn,
> the trees bear up their ruin,
>   and everything nudges our lives towards the coming ash.
>   ('Via Negativa', *A Short History of the Shadow*

This new concision allows some longer narrative threads to break into impressionistic blocks, and Wright has admitted the influence of Cezanne on his layering technique. This can result in short passages which are, at surface, more easily accessible than the longer journal sequences, meaning that later collections are both manageable and can access sudden profundity. Nevertheless, there are recurring features jutting out of this landscape: his poems inevitably find him out late in his backyard, looking up and noting the constellations, or ruminating on friends last seen years ago in Italy: it is a given, just as much as his sense of cosmic fatalism, shading into wry joking acceptance (in a way not dissimilar to, but less surreal than, his friend Charles Simic).

Wright is on record as being preoccupied with form over content, and the late collection *Sestets* (2009) differs from much of his work, taking his playfulness even more concision, being composed throughout in single, seven-line stanzas:

Tutti Frutti

> 'A-wop-bop-a-loo-lop-a-lop-bam-boo',
>   Little Richard in full gear-
> What could be better than that?
> Not much that I know of, at least not in my green time.

> It's hard. O my, it is hard,
> To find a sustainable ecstasy, and make it endure.
> Detail, detail, detail-God and the Devil
>   hang side by side between each break.

This substantial distillation of Wright's work – some way short of a *Collected Poems* – charts his determined struggle to maintain such a sustainable ecstasy; it is poetry full of luminous light and wry, dark humour wrestled out of a serious, almost priestly approach.

Palimpsest of Ghosts

Abigail Chabitnoy, *How to Dress a Fish* (Wesleyan) £11.50

Reviewed by DAVID C. WARD

In 2018 the Smithsonian's National Museum of the American Indian (NMAI) opened an exhibition called, with nicely understated but pointed humour, 'Americans' that dwelt on the paradox that Indians are everywhere in American culture but nowhere are there actual historical or contemporary Indians. In fact that should be 'Indians' because they appear as subjects of cultural and economic appropriation, deracinated and de-historicized so that they appear only as symbols: trade marks (Indian motorcycles), sports nicknames (most odiously the Washington Redskins), or brand names (Tomahawk missiles) and so on. Indians only have a currency if their actual Indian-ness is whitewashed away, sometimes literally, as in the portraits of the Indian maiden Pochantas. NMAI, in its other exhibitions, has a curatorial policy of preferring not to display images of Indians or Indian life by non-Indians. As an historian I think it's instructive to interrogate how the oppressor conceived or visualized you but for a relatively new museum the imperative to have Indians define themselves is politically and emotionally understandable.

Yet the question, which is not singular to the history of American Indians but shared by many groups that history has rolled over, of how one recovers and reconstitutes past time, remains a vital question. Abigail Chabitony, an Aleut who lives in Alaska, in her remarkable book, *How to Dress a Fish* grapples with her family history, and by implication the history of all Native Peoples, to reassemble the unstable and conjectural fragments of a past that has left only archeological tracings. Her book centres around the recovery of the life of her great grandfather Michael, orphaned in the first decade of the 20th century and taken from Alaska to the Indian College in Carlisle Pennsylvania (known now mostly as the home of the great athlete Jim Thorpe). The book is dedicated, plaintively, to Michael: 'it didn't feel right / I couldn't see you / Is this the shape these things should take.' Michael's story begins with FAMILY ~~GHOSTS~~ HISTORY in the form of a college form filling in his family details. Chabitnoy doesn't say whether this is a real or imagined form, one that she has put together from the details that are known to her. Uncertainty is her point. Everything is questionable – and questioned: 'Father. Dead. *Yes.* Traumatized. / Mother. Dead. *Yes.* Heart Trouble. (bad heart.)' 'Traumatized' meaning what exactly? Killed by history? The replication of the form ends with an entry dated 10 April 1909: 'Student. *Michael Chabitnoy*. Nation, *Aleut*. went on an outing and did not return.' I like this: laconic in its bureaucratese it reverses a whole theme of American literature and the white man lighting out for the territories. Instead it is the Indian who leaves 'civilization'. But where did he go? In her next text, Chabitnoy follows the official appearance of her college form with scribbled genealogical notes and speculations about her family on a shopping list (*'eggs/apples/bananas'*) including the lines:

– no one really told stories about
  'the Indian'
pic on train w/ 'Jim Thorpe' face
rubbed out

A few Indians are allowed to become famous, but the rest are rubbed out, commodified in some way, shape or form, as the exhibition 'Americans' documents. And all Indians also become totems of every other Indian: all Indians are 'Jim Thorpe' or Pocahontas or Sitting Bull. Who was Michael though? In her great grandfather's section, Chabitnoy several times uses the typographical device of a rectangular empty box on the page. A blank space to be filled in, a tabula rasa, or a space which nothing will ever fill? One blank box is headed 'OBSERVE THE INDIAN AS SUBJECT'. Notice the anthropological phrasing: the subject of others.

These two documents set up the rest of the book and Chabitnoy fills in the blank spaces with poetry that is both specific to her family and the history of American Indians (especially the fur trade and savage relations with the Russians) but also connects with ancient myths Greek as well as Native, particularly origin myths about water which are the subjects of section two. Fish appear, particularly sharks and salmon; the original 'Shebutnoy' was apparently Russian for 'Salmon-fisher', or was it?

Because it doesn't mean *salmon-fisher*.
Because I need to know I can say these words.
Because it means 'mischevious, energetic'.
Mischevious men (and women) fish for salmon energetically.

The question of genealogy and self-discovery runs through the book: 'I will split my bones and fit my skin to the sea. / I will shape my mouth to angle these words with the wind.' There's a nice double meaning on angle / angling. On the one hand, pushing against the prevailing wind that wipes things clear and, on the other fishing for the past and the original fisherman, her great grandfather.

Yet Chabitnoy resists easy answers or constructing some kind of nice story about finding her ancestors. Michael remains a mystery, visible only in glimpses: a photograph, an official note, family legend. A triptych of poems charts the disintegration of the historical subject: FAMILY HISTORY beings:

Only the beginning is true.

there was an island
and an orphanage
and a boy.

FAMILY STORY

    the beginning is true
  There was

    a boy.

And the third poem disintegrates further. M Y STORY: 'Only // beginning is true /// an island /// a boy. /// a train a country.' Chabitnoy pushes against what she cannot find, some rootedness against the past's displacements of her family, some connective genealogy that she can only explicate or speak into being through her poems. In the southwestern 'Four Corners' she looks for the so-called authentic Indian experience, finding it mostly in the gift shops, while looking for Warhol's 'commodified Indian to hang / on my wall'. A mordant joke resonating with NMAI's 'Americans' exhibition: an image paid for in blood. Poems too are found there.

Looking at the Walls

David Van-Cauter, *Mirror Lake*
(Arenig), £5.99; Hilary Menos, *Human
Tissue* (Smith Doorstop), £6; Vicki
Husband, *Sykkel Saga* (Mariscat) £6

Reviewed by RORY WATERMAN

What, when we turn from the news and pick up one of
the many books we are locked away with, doesn't seem
tempered by current events, or riddled with dramatic
ironies? When I read 'I close the door and try to concen-
trate' – the only one-line stanza in the first poem of David
Van-Cauter's *Mirror Lake* – I am not transported, but
brought back thumpingly to a global predicament his
pamphlet could not have foreseen. I turn my eyes from
the page, and back to the screen.

It is hardly Van-Cauter's fault, of course, and his poems
repay closer attention. *Mirror Lake* is lively, sometimes
light-hearted and often very moving, even when rooting
around in what appears to be the author's deep store of
quotidian experiences. That opening poem, 'Piano', is a
subtle, pitch-perfect lyric not so much about putting up
with someone else's foibles, as embracing them – so
perhaps after all it does have something to teach us in
our current shared moment:

> *Sorry, was I disturbing you?*
> *No, no,* I say. *Keep playing.*
>
> I walk into the kitchen
> listen to you begin
> that first, inquiring hum
> that softer, timid touch.

Several of these disparate poems are concerned with
the death of a partner. In these, the persistently calm
warmth of Van-Cauter's voice, and his skill at handling
delays and surges of thought with line-breaks, serves to
make his miniature narratives all the more affecting, as
he focuses on the shoes that 'made their way to charity
shops: / other walks, other homes', or itemises what has
changed in a local delicatessen: 'the menu doesn't fold
/ the way it used to', and he waits 'a beat too long / for
you to emerge' from the bathroom. These are plain-speak-
ing poems, free of ostensible linguistic fireworks, but
full of subtexts and other hard-won intricacies of thought
and feeling.

The title poem, named for the famous seasonal lake
in Yosemite National Park, remembers when 'we took
the "easy route" to Mirror Lake, / you still fit enough to
clamber over rocky paths for miles', and ends with a
return that cannot come full circle:

> Mirror Lake consumes us in its folds,
> as if I'm the one who died and you're still alive,
> walking backwards to seek out this place
> ten years from now, remembering how
> life suddenly dried up, absorbing us.

This is significantly more powerful than the pamphlet's
few other poems of travel, most of which do little but
sketch their location, albeit vividly. Some of Van-Cauter's
epiphanies are also a bit much – as in 'A Flight', which
feels artificially spellbound by the magic of an invention
more than a century old. But even most of the pamphlet's
pithier pieces show an impressive knack for witty encap-
sulations of human nature, often matched with a tricksy
use of formal constraints. In 'Hoem', for example, he
turns a neat sonnet ironically against itself, and his aspi-
rations towards some of its most lauded practitioners,
in a depiction of home-hunting: 'we could buy a place in
Byron Close [...] / Keats Way felt romantic', but 'you said /
to focus on the house and not the name', so 'I started
looking at the walls instead: / these things enclose us all'.
Again, I am thrown into our present elongated moment.
Never were truer words said. Van-Cauter's generous
poems might be especially welcome now, and help many
of us to put our shared concerns in context.

The same might be said of Hilary Menos's *Human Tis-
sue*. This pamphlet – a long sequence, really – is dedicat-
ed to a child:

> I fold the corner of the page to mark our place
> and smooth the hair from a sleeping face.
> Nobody knows how a story ends.

There are too many poems about parenthood, an expe-
rience as apparently magical for those experiencing it as
it is typically boring for everyone else when poured into
epiphanic poetry. But this isn't the usual paean. Menos's
son Linus, the dedicatee, suffered kidney failure, and
took one of his mother's kidneys – 'your kidney / which
I am keeping warm' – in what at first appeared to be a
successful transplant. Two years later, his body rejected
it, and he went on dialysis. This pamphlet documents
these experiences, sometimes aslant and sometimes head
on, with an acuity available only to a genuinely superb
poet with a heightened passion for her subject. The result
is one of the most moving, stylish and, indeed, life-
affirming pamphlets I have read in years.

Melos isn't a formalist, but her poems often suddenly
click into subtle metre and rhyme at just the right
moment. Sometimes she uses curtal lines, though she
never over-does the trick, so its surprise doesn't wear off.
'Oblatory', a poem in step with traditions and seasonal
shifts, ends with a present attempt at respite, and a rev-
erie of the past:

> I kneel and rest my forehead on the ground
>
> and remember another time, another place.
> Your first smile. Your lit face.

And in 'Admission':

> I write a letter to you, at home with our son,
> and bury it deep in my notebook
> between special diets and test results and plans
> where only you would look
>
> Just in case anything goes wrong.
> *Up at six, down at eight, out by twelve, recovery till two.*
> I'm counting hours. It won't be long.
> *I love you.*

The pamphlet's two powerful leitmotifs, playing fugue to the main narrative, are icons of Christian faith (viewed with some irony), and the 'Mud Man' who 'squats in the copse, / his one long leg slung out like a telegraph pole', and 'looks at me through struck flint eyes': 'We must feed him every weekend, says my son, / and we do'. Occasionally, these streams of thought come into temporary confluence: 'The Mud Man believes in revelation', though he 'does not expect to find what he seeks in any cathedral / but out here'. It does him no good: towards the end of the pamphlet he is 'gone, replaced by an access road', 'a spatter of sawdust where we used to sit', and 'a smear of part-digested sloe berries': 'Sometimes trees are just trees, mud is mud'. The pamphlet ends with 'Sloe Gin', a poem of meditation and ritual, a lesson in faltering onwards, dressed up as a set of instructions:

> Sloes are defiant fruit, each one hard won.
> Walk home the long way, clutching your pot or pan
>
> And sobbing. Guidance. I'd hoped to give you more.
> Add sugar and gin. Shake. Store.
>
> Time matures the thing. At least, adds distance.

Even when this lockdown ends and we are permitted once more to go about infecting one another – a policy we should not forget our government endorsing as recently as the middle of March – I don't suppose many of us will be itching to propel ourselves along approximately 400 miles of underused Arctic byway. Vicki Husband's *Sykkel Saga*, a long poem mainly in sprightly free-verse tercets with occasional determined forays away from the safety rail of the left-hand margin, is a celebration of taking to the open road through northern Norway on two wheels. (If you're especially clever – or Norwegian, I suppose – you will already have worked out that a sykkel is a cycle.)

The poem is to some extent a fragmented trip through Norse mythology as well as through wild *landskap* and past *fjelltoppene*; Husband provides a handy glossary of her borrowings, and another of characters from Norse mythology. Most of all, though, this is a travel diary shaped into verse, and a celebration of unusual experience in the first person, so that we might feel some of the freewheeling for ourselves, and some of the bumps in the road. Despite the 'blasted teeth of rock', vivid 'Mustard, paprika / houses' that 'seed the *fjord* sides', and birds that 'unpick the sky', the poem is equally concerned with being constantly aware of one's body as it is with fells, farms, fjords, and fowl:

> My heart rate settles
> to a jagged trace,
>
> a mountain range, peak/
> pigg and trough; my blood travels
> much further than me.

> Each slim pass we crest,
> then slip as through the waist
> of an hourglass.

That 'further' should really be 'farther', but the epiphany is well handled, the images lithe and apt. The wide-eyed wonder is very occasionally nauseating – these holiday-makers, we are told, are 'pilgrims to an / exotic idea' – but more often than not the language is precise and pleasing enough to allow vicarious pleasure in the adventure. When you can't go beyond the local park (or even perhaps into it) you might as well enjoy someone else's limpid account of doing so.

SOME CONTRIBUTORS

Diana Bridge's seventh collection of poems, *Two or more islands*, was published by Otago UP last year. She has a background in Chinese literature and art history and recently completed a collaborative translation of a selection of classical poems. Raised in Jamaica, **Christine Roseeta Walker** holds a Masters in Creative Writing. She is a poet and novelist whose work vividly captures the extraordinary experiences of life in the Caribbean. **Lucy Cheseldine** in a PhD candidate at the University of Leeds. She has studied Literature in Glasgow, Dublin, and the United States. She is a regular contributor to Stand magazine and her poetry has appeared in Eborakon. **Jenny King** has written poetry since childhood. She has published three pamphlets, one in 1981 with Mandeville Press and now two with The Poetry Business. She lives in Sheffield. **Katerina Anghelaki-Rooke** was born in Athens, Greece, and died 20 January, 2020 at the age of eighty-one. She is the author of more than twenty books of poetry and numerous translations (Pushkin, Plath, Heaney). Her own work has been translated into more than a dozen languages. She won the Greek National Poetry Prize (1985), the Academy's Poetry Prize (2000) and the National Lifetime Achievement in Literature Prize (2014). Her home was on the island of Aegina. **Karen Van Dyck** is the Kimon A. Doukas Professor of Modern Greek Literature in the Classics Department at Columbia University. Her translations include *The Scattered Papers of Penelope*, an edited collection of the poetry of Katerina Anghelaki-Rooke (Graywolf 2009*), Austerity Measures: The New Greek Poetry* (NYRB 2017, winner of the London Hellenic Prize), and Margarita Liberaki's novel *Three Summers* (NYRB 2019). **Tara Bergin** wrote her PhD on the process and influence of poetic translation, a topic which has preoccupied much of her writing since. She has published two collections with Carcanet Press, *This is Yarrow* (2013) and *The Tragic Death of Eleanor Marx* (2017). **Leo Boix** is a bilingual poet born in Argentina who lives in the UK. He is the recipient of the Keats-Shelley Prize 2019. Boix debut collection will be published by Chatto & Windus in 2021. **Tony Roberts**'s fifth collection, *The Noir American & Other Poems*, was published in 2018. His second book of essays on poets, poetry and critics, *The Taste of My Mornings*, appeared in 2019. Both are from Shoestring Press. **Carol Rumens**'s latest collections is *The Mixed Urn* (Sheep Meadow Press, 2019). Her pamphlet *Bezdelki: Small Things*, illustrated by Emma Wright (The Emma Press*)*, won a Michael Marks Award in 2018. **Aram Saroyan**'s 'New Drawings', curated by Michael Ned Holte, was seen at the As-Is LA Gallery in January and February 2020. Working primarily as an artist in recent years, examples of Saroyan's work can be seen on Instagram at saroyanesque. **Martin Caseley** contributes regular essays, articles and book reviews to several journals, including *Agenda* and *PN Review*. He lives in Norfolk and also writes book reviews for the *International Times* and *Stride* websites. Recent pieces have covered the music of Ronnie Lane, Clive James, Thomas Hardy and Alison Brackenbury. **Walter Bruno** taught literature, film, drama, and communications until retirement. In addition to critical commentary, he has put out collections of his poetry. His latest volume is *First Declension: new and collected poems.* **Martin Elliott** is a one-time bookseller, a quondam academic, an erstwhile civil servant. Author of Shakespeare's *Invention of Othello* (Macmillan) and stories in *London Magazine, Encounter, New Review & LRB.* **Caroline Maldonado**'s translations from Italian include poems by Rocco Scotellaro *Your call keeps us awake (2013)*, Isabella Morra *Isabella* (2019), Laura Fusco, *Liminal,* (2020) all published by Smokestack Books. **J. Kates** is a poet and literary translator who lives in Fitzwilliam, New Hampshire. **Suzannah V. Evans**'s debut double-pamphlet *Marine Objects / Some Language* is published with Guillemot Press. **David C. Ward** is Senior Historian *emeritus,* National Portrait Gallery, Smithsonian Institution. His *Call Waiting* was published by Carcanet in 2014.

COLOPHON

Editors
Michael Schmidt
Andrew Latimer

Associate Editor
Charlotte Rowland

Design
Cover and Typesetting
by Andrew Latimer

Editorial address
The Editors at the address
on the right. Manuscripts
cannot be returned unless
accompanied by a stamped
addressed envelope or
international reply coupon.

Trade distributors
NBN International (orders)
10 Thornbury Road, PL6 7PP
orders@nbninternational.com

Represented by
Compass IPS Ltd
Great West House
Brentford, TW8 9DF, UK
sales@compassips.london

Copyright
© 2020 Poetry Nation Review
All rights reserved
ISBN 978-1-78410-832-8
ISSN 0144-7076

Subscriptions (6 issues)
INDIVIDUALS (print and digital):
   £39.50; abroad £49
INSTITUTIONS (print only): £76;
   abroad £90
INSTITUTIONS (digital):
   subscriptions from Exact Editions
   (https://shop.exacteditions.com/
   gb/pn-review)
to: *PN Review*, Alliance House,
   30 Cross Street, Manchester
   M2 7AQ, UK

Supported by